A MIND OF ITS OWN

A MIND OF ITS OWN

*Healing the Mind and Heart
of the
Parasite of Childhood Abuse*

John J. Lemoncelli, Ed.D.

AVENTURA
PRESS
Eynon, PA

ISBN-13: 978-0-9761553-4-8
Published by
Avventura Press
133 Handley St.
Eynon PA 18403-1305
570-876-5817
www.avventurapress.com

1st printing September 2008

Printed in the United States of America

DEDICATION

HAPPY ARE THOSE WHO DREAM DREAMS

AND ARE WILLING TO PAY THE PRICE

TO MAKE THEM COME TRUE.

—*L.J. Cardinal Suenens*

To God, who, through grace, has shown me the "magic"
people possess
when we will to dream.

To my mother, Jean, deceased father, "Pop" Sam and sister
Cathy, who, by their love, encouragement, gentleness and
faith, have given me life's greatest gift:
The gift of being able to dream.

To our children, Mark and Mauri, who, by their love,
laughter, sincerity and zeal for life, have given me life's
greatest treasure:
*The treasure of having the faith and hope to believe in
dreams.*

To my bride and best friend, Maggie, who, by her love,
strength, encouragement, hope and humor, has shared with
me life's most challenging task:
The task of making dreams come true.

To you, my family, the source of my strength and purpose,
because you so willingly, unselfishly, and lovingly
paid the price:
*This dream is dedicated with gratitude, humility and
much love.*

ACKNOWLEDGEMENTS

After submitting the manuscript to the publisher, I began to contemplate the many people who encouraged, supported, or contributed to my research over the past years. I realized that if I were to acknowledge each person individually, the acknowledgements would be longer than the text. So, to those people who are not mentioned individually, especially my clients, I want you all to know how grateful I am to you. To all the following people, I want to say a tremendous heartfelt "Thank you for everything!"

All of my patients who over the course of many years taught me so much.....

All my graduate assistants, especially Meaghan Broderick, Susan Thompson, Danielle Fleming and Rebecca Cohen.....

Drs. Stephen Southern, Henry Smorenski, James Gearity, Lois Draina, and Mary Ann Fedrick, who assisted me in developing the interplay of scholarship and practice.....

Guido D. Boriosi, M.D., who has been my mentor in private practice.....

Anthony A. Galdieri, Ph.D., my colleague, my sounding board, my dear friend who has made our work a joy.....

Dr. Samuel Knapp, a friend and true inspiration.....

Carmen Ambrozino, a "gentle" man who taught me to laugh, and who is always there for us.....

Lee and Lori Sebastiani, who were always encouraging.....

Toni (T.J.) Jones, who is always an enormous support to both me and my family.....

My mom, our children, and especially my wife who are incredible supports.....

I know I could have not done this without all of you.

Deo gratias!!

FOREWORD

Over my years in private practice, I have never come across a book as creative and easy to understand as Dr. John Lemoncelli's *A Mind of Its Own: Healing the Mind and Heart of the Parasite of Childhood Abuse.* Practical and concise, *A Mind of Its Own* offers abuse victims essential guidance on how to identify abuse, the need to acknowledge the pain they are experiencing, and becoming a survivor.

On a broad level, Dr. Lemoncelli likens child abuse to a parasite invading its host. The parasite-concept turns child abuse into a concrete, tangible idea that the victim can see, understand, grasp onto, and develop strategies to combat. In practice, the therapist would change the victim's perspective through supportive therapy: to help clients identify the parasite and attempt to minimize it so it no longer creates pain.

At a theoretical level, the parasite-concept relies on psychological and biological principles as well as the Alcoholic's Anonymous Twelve Step program to help the victim develop strategies to cope with abuse. These principles are then bound together by a strong overtone of spirituality to become the foundation on which the parasite-concept rests.

As a well-respected teacher and private practitioner, John Lemoncelli has been treating abuse victims using this parasite-concept for years with much success. It is a simple, easy-to-use process that works. In this area of psychotherapy, Dr. Lemoncelli enjoys an excellent reputation which will only continue to grow.

Anthony A. Galdieri, Ph.D.
Licensed Psychologist

CONTENTS

An invitation to clinicians...

If you have been or are currently treating adults who are survivors of childhood abuse, you know all too well the devastation abuse has on a person's total being. I have been treating adult survivors for twenty-plus years. After attending all the seminars and reading most, if not all, of the books, the struggle with my own ineptness continued. I found myself feeling that this abuse or something about the abuse almost had a mind or life of its own. This abuse thing was cunning and powerful, yet, I had no idea what the thing was.

In this text, I have proposed that the "abuse thing" is similar to a Parasite in the human psyche. The Parasite is ingested into a child as contaminated love. The Parasite, then, causes ego fragmentation. This ego fragmentation, which is maintained by the Parasite, creates an abuse-pain, abuse-pain cycle. Thus our clients continue on a journey of self abuse and self loathing. The Parasite model which I detail in this text affords our clients with the opportunity to attack something other than themselves.

Since the early days of my career, the disease model employed in the drug and alcohol field has intrigued me. Over the course of my clinical investigation of the Parasite theory, I have also incorporated the disease model into this theory. Numerous AA principles have also been incorporated into the theory in order to aide patients in their treatment.

For the past fifteen years, I have been utilizing the treatment model contained in this text. The response from patients has been gratifying and enlightening. Patients tell me over and over again how much sense the Parasite theory and treatment model makes to them, and that it affords patients much realistic hope.

This Parasite theory and treatment model has been presented at state, regional and national conferences. The response from our colleagues has been most positive. However, in terms of a true investigation into the efficacy of this Parasite theory and treatment model, I have only case examples. The number of cases to date, given the complexity of abuse, is not sufficient for hypothesis testing. Furthermore, the limitation of experimenter bias is obvious. I believe this theory is valid and I know the treatment model works.

This text was written not to present all the answers, but rather to begin the questioning process in order to conduct a true investigation into the universal applicability of the Parasite theory and treatment model. My true aspiration is that this text serves as an introduction into the process to facilitate our dialogue. I welcome you to fully engage in this dialogue with me. Currently a website is being developed through the publisher where we can examine the strengths and weaknesses of the Parasite theory and treatment model. Hopefully, we, together, will develop an empirically validated treatment protocol for this incredibly painful epidemic trauma.

For information about bulk sales of *A Mind of Its Own*, please contact Avventura Press at 570-876-5817 or email lee@avventurapress.com

www.avventurapress.com

Introduction

I am writing this book in the hope that it will somehow help you in your struggle recovering from the horrible trauma of abuse. It is written directly to you, the victim, to clear the way to understanding. I have seen the pain on the faces of so many of my patients, and have been privileged to journey with them on their road to recovery. They have taught me so much and helped me to help them. I have learned how important it is that someone appreciated how twisted and torn they have felt for years. I believe I have come to know how vital that validation is to them and to you.

What is contained in this text is one man's heartfelt attempt to help you sort out what has happened to you because of the trauma you experienced. More importantly, I want to share with you concepts that have helped hundreds of my patients curtail many of their self-abusing behaviors and become true survivors of abuse. So, then, the emphasis of this text will be directed at appreciating *what has happened* and learning *how to* ease some, if not all, of the devastating pain your trauma has caused. Unfortunately, the burning question you probably have—"Why?" or "Why Me?"—will not be answered.

Several years ago, Rabbi Kushner wrote a book entitled *When Bad Things Happen to Good People*. While the Rabbi is a much more learned man than I am, he really didn't come up with an ultimate answer. So the answer to the "Why?/Why Me?" question is, regrettably, that I don't know. But what I do know is that *you* are not responsible! *You* are not damaged! *You* are not a horrible person! Perhaps life is more a roll of the dice than we want to imagine. Perhaps some day, if there is a Creator, the Creator will fully explain that haunting "Why/Why Me?" puzzle. But for now, suffice it to say that someone or something in your life path chose to participate in evil and to violate your personhood.

I will attempt to help you appreciate how this violation of personhood or violation of boundaries created numerous difficulties in your growth and development. This will be detailed in chapter two, which concerns the impact of abuse on child development. Dr. Andy Carey and I first published an article on this subject in 1996. While I believe that much, if not all, of what we theorized then remains true today, we had yet to comprehend an essential aspect of the abuse cycle.

The theory outlined in this text is based on solid principles from the fields of biology and psychology, and from the tenets of the Alcoholics Anonymous Twelve Step program. Taken individually, these concepts are both readily understood and quite valid. When put together, though, the result might raise an eyebrow or two. Yet, when I introduced these concepts to my patients, the concepts appeared to make perfect sense to them. I believe we need to explore how to incorporate these various concepts because the problem of child abuse is so complex.

The Alcoholics Anonymous Twelve Step program has been around since 1935, and has helped millions of people on their journey in recovering from their addiction. More recently, psychology has begun to recognize that addiction can and does go beyond alcohol and drugs. Psychology now recognizes gambling, pornography, sex, and food (to name a few) as having a true addictive nature. However, psychology, for the most part, has failed to genuinely incorporate the Twelve Step concepts into traditional mental health treatment. You might ask, "Why is this important?" Because all of the patients that I have seen who were victims of abuse were, at some point, addicted to self-abusive behaviors. Here is where I would ask you to be gut honest. Are you engaging in self-abusive behaviors? Do you allow others to continue to violate your personal boundaries? Do you constantly beat yourself up with negative thoughts about yourself? AA refers to negative self talk as "stinking thinking." The concepts of the Twelve Step program have a great deal to offer victims of child abuse. No, you don't have to go to meetings, unless there is another addiction—but it couldn't hurt!

The Twelve Step programs have also adopted a "disease model" for their fellowship. Do you feel sick inside most of the time? Then perhaps abuse creates a kind of illness: an illness that you can work at putting in remission. An illness that you can fight against, rather than fighting against yourself.

I know well the great "illness" debates that occur in the mental health community. These debates have been with us since the 1970s. As a psychologist, I must admit that I, too, was most skeptical regarding the adoption of the illness model to mental health issues. Does an illness model basically say you just need to take these pills or those pills to get well? Does the illness model take away the responsibility to actively do things to become well? The answer to these questions is a resounding *no!* In the Twelve Step model, the person is most definitely responsible to work a program in order to be in recovery. The illness model holds the person responsible to work at recovery, but also respects the concept that no one sets out to become an alcoholic or drug addict. Genetics, circumstances, and/or the desire to self-medicate pain can result in addiction or illness. No one sets out to become a victim of abuse.

Similarly, the illness model that I'm proposing holds you responsible to work at your recovering. You, unfortunately, can't just take pills and make it all go away. I wish you could. No, you will need to struggle and work your program in order to be a true survivor. However, you are not responsible for becoming ill. You didn't ask for it. You did nothing to precipitate that kind of behavior from the abuser. You are not damaged goods. You did not desire this abuse. You may have wanted the abuser to love you. NOT like that! You may have wanted the abuser to touch you. NOT there! NOT like that! You may have wanted to feel special to someone. NOT that way! You are NOT responsible for the abuse, but something inside you makes you feel that you are. That is your disease. That is the "thing" with which you must struggle.

But, what is this *thing* that creates these horrible feelings? What seems to seduce you into self-destructive, self-abusive behaviors? Time and time again I have heard from my patients, "It was like something came over me."

"It was like something baited me into this situation."

"Is there something bad inside of me?"

For many years, I wasn't sure what to say to answer these questions. Then, I began to adopt the disease model and would simply say, "It's your disease." This seemed to engender more questions from my patients. "But what kind of disease? How do I get rid of it?" I have felt for a long time that this disease, this *thing* seemed to have a kind of mind of its own. This *thing* was shrewd, cunning, and appeared a great deal wilier than me.

I then began to look to biology in order to attempt to better understand this *thing* and to create a metaphor to help my patients and me better understand their disease. I researched viruses and bacteria and came upon the literature concerning parasites. Parasites enter a healthy host organism and infiltrate various parts of the host organism. Parasites exist for two reasons: 1) to consume the host, and 2) to replicate themselves. This *thing*, your disease, your illness, is metaphorically a *Parasite*. It has entered into your system as contaminated love. It infiltrated your thoughts and your feelings. If it has its way, it will invade your psyche—your soul—and consume the host. It will destroy the good person that you are.

How many victims have destroyed themselves, either overtly or covertly? Has the Parasite ever consumed the host? Unfortunately, from my vantage point, the answer is *yes*. I have experienced patients overtly destroying themselves through completed suicide. I have also witnessed patients lose all hope and become consumed by their pain. They continue in self-destructive, self-abasing behaviors and covertly destroy themselves. And what about the people who truly care about this victim who destroyed the self? Those people feel complete helplessness and hopelessness witnessing their loved one destroy the self. Has, indeed, the Parasite now replicated itself in them?

I realize what you have just read can be quite startling. I am not attempting to frighten you or to tempt you into thinking that I'm crazy. I am attempting to help you see that you need not give this Parasite one more day of your life. I also have presented this to reinforce that YOU are not crazy either; you are not damaged; you are not a bad person. You have an illness from which you begin recovering today. Today is the first day of the rest of YOUR life.

Perhaps we should stop here. If this model that I have presented doesn't really fit for you, that's really not a problem. I'm sure that some of my fellow psychologists might have grave difficulty with some of the concepts. If you are in therapy and it's working, keep doing what you are doing. If you are not in therapy and this does not fit for you, you need to find a psychologist or counselor who is less eclectic. Perhaps a pure cognitive behaviorist would be helpful. The important thing is that you get help. You need not bear your pain alone. It can be too heavy a load. The New Testament tells us that the Christ fell under the weight of His cross. He needed a Simon, a stranger, to help Him with the heavy load. A therapist can be your Simon. The therapist can help you bear the weight of YOUR cross.

Suppose, though, that this *does* make sense to you and you are already in therapy. I suggest you share this approach with your therapist, particularly if you are feeling bogged down. You and your therapist may like some aspects. That's great. Use what is helpful, and discard the rest. Again, the important thing is that you keep working your program. Remember, "It works if you work it, so work it, you're worth it."

Let's look more closely at this Parasite. Image yourself at the age when the abuse began. Someone you trusted, a parent, neighbor or family member, handed you a glass of water. It looked cool and refreshing and you were thirsty. You drank the water and it felt good. Then the person told you never to tell anyone about the glass of water. Suddenly you began to feel bad inside. You know the story all too well. The water which you thought was nourishing was contaminated; this is the beginning of the illness.

Think about this. As a child you trusted the abuser. The abuser gave you contaminated love. You did not know it was contaminated. How could you know? The contamination began to make you feel ill. You perhaps looked to the abuser for more love to make you feel better. And the abuser gave you more of this poisoned love. You may have felt dirty, ashamed, or even guilty. The more ill you felt, the more you needed love to make you feel better. Then you got even more contaminated love. Perhaps, for a moment, you even felt better. Perhaps you enjoyed the moment, or just felt special, only to feel, later, even more ill. As time went on, the Parasite grew stronger, infiltrating more of the parts of your self. Even now, the Parasite plays with your thoughts and your feelings. Every day you are at war with yourself. And the war doesn't seem to ever stop!

Let me give you an example. Jane is a twenty-five year old professional single woman. She was the eldest of three siblings, having two younger sisters. Jane was sexually abused by her biological father from age ten to fourteen. In spite of the abuse, she was a star athlete in high school and a straight A-student. She graduated from college summa cum laude, and is very successful at her job. A perfectionist and a people pleaser, she has been dating Tim, who might be described as... a loser. He can't keep a job, drinks too much and has been verbally and physically abusive to Jane. Jane has vowed to herself that she must not see him anymore. Two weeks ago she broke off the relationship, but tonight she is feeling very lonely. In her head the Parasite baits her. "He is okay. He's nice most of the time," etc., etc. She goes to see him. He has his way with her, and then treats her like a tramp. On the way home, in tears and devastated, the Parasite plays with her again. "You stupid jackass. What the hell is wrong with you? You are damaged. You asked for it," and on and on.

There are so many examples, like Jane, where the Parasite plays both sides of the person. The tragedy is that the individual always loses.

I have actually attempted to envision what the Parasite might look like. (Perhaps I have too much time on my hands? Oh, well.) As I see it, it has numerous tentacles much like an octopus. The tentacles infect the various parts of your *cognitions* (thoughts) and the various parts of your *affect* (emotions.) It has one eye and that is where it is vulnerable. Therapy needs to be directed at the eye, rather than simply attacking the tentacles infecting the parts. In this way, therapy would be metaphorically likened to radiation therapy—very directed, with little damage to the good cells. The eye is simply the ability to identify when the Parasite is playing the person into thinking and/or feeling in a self destructive, self-abusive manner. I believe that therapy that does not identify the Parasite is much more metaphorically like chemotherapy, which destroys good cells along with the bad.

Traditional talk or verbal therapy demands good communication skills. It is essential that both the therapist and patient are able to understand what the other is saying. Implicit in this understanding is the accurate meaning of the words both therapist and patient are using. Too often, we use various words that have specific meaning to us, but may not have the same meaning to another person. In order to provide clarity between you, the reader, and me regarding the meaning of various words, I will use very specific definitions. I hope this will assist you in capturing the full meaning of the essential terms I will use.

Throughout this book I will be using actual case examples. These have been appropriately disguised to protect the identity of my active or former clients. Some of the case examples might even represent composites of several patients. Nonetheless, the case examples are true to the spirit of the issues involved. I would also like to share with you that these generous and courageous individuals have signed releases of information for their stories to be included in this text. It is also their hope that their pain will be used to help you conquer yours. The majority of the case examples represent sexual abuse in order to demonstrate the model of the Parasite clearly. The research to date indicates that sexual abuse typically comprises both physical and emotional abuse. Please keep in mind that abuse stretches across the continuum and by no means am I attempting to minimize the significance of physical and/or emotional abuse.

In the next chapter we will discuss the Parasite in more detail. You will notice that there is some redundancy throughout this text. This isn't done just to fill more pages. It is purposeful, because you will need a certain amount of redundancy to achieve true understanding and to help alter your thoughts, feelings, and eventually behavior patterns. Be as patient as you can. AA says, "Keep coming back. If you bring the body, the mind will follow."

1

THE WORKINGS OF THE PARASITE

Let us begin with an examination of how some theoreticians view abuse. Actually, there are some theoreticians who see emotional, physical, and sexual abuse as all being different. There are other theoreticians who see abuse on a continuum, each producing a different level of trauma. The latter is how I view abuse. Many times the victim may experience all three types of abuse. Whatever type or level of abuse that you have endured, the key is never to minimize the pain that has been engendered by that abuse. Many times I hear victims saying to me, and more importantly, to themselves, "Well, it could have been worse. I'm sure there are people out there who have experienced more significant trauma." This definitely is what I would term a Parasitic mantra. This mantra causes you to minimize your pain and subsequently suppress it. The result is that you do not validate your pain. Without appropriate and thorough validation, the victim remains stuck in his or her feelings.

Validation of your feelings is the first step in truly coping with them. The feelings may be quite uncomfortable. The feelings, in your mind, may even be morally wrong. You need to remember you have a right to have them. Whenever I discuss feelings with both my students and patients, I ask them to always remember the two R's in feelings:

Right to feel the feelings, and

Responsibility to cope with the feelings in a socially, morally and legally appropriate fashion.

You may feel you want to hurt your abuser the way you were hurt. You have the right to this feeling, and the responsibility to cope with that feeling in an appropriate manner. You do not have the right to inflict bodily harm on your abuser, regardless of how you feel. But, you do have the right to feel. Once your pain is appropriately validated, you can then begin to cope with that feeling.

Many people attempt to use minimization to assist them in coping with difficult feelings. If a person is attempting to use minimization without first appropriately validating the pain, it is like putting the cart before the horse. You are going nowhere and will get stuck in your feelings. I worked with a young man named Jim who was physically and emotionally abused by his father. Jim recounted numerous times how his father would come home in violent rages. Jim's father was an avid sportsman who possessed numerous weapons. It was not uncommon for him to chase Jim and his brothers around the house with a loaded gun. The father even discharged the weapon inside the home. When Jim revealed the details of the abuse, I could see the terror on his face. I could hear the total disbelief in his voice. Without identifying and validating his feelings, Jim would immediately minimize the feeling. He would often say, "Well, he didn't shoot any of us. He only shot at the walls or the ceiling. It could have been worse." Yes, it could have been worse, and putting the abuse in perspective may have helped Jim to cope with his feelings. But the minimization, his attempt to place the abuse in perspective, kept Jim stuck in those terrible feelings. He needed to validate his feelings in order to begin coping with them.

Whatever experiences you have had to endure, the initial key is the validation of your pain. I use this example with my patients in therapy. Suppose we are soldiers in Baghdad and our vehicle hits a mine. The soldier next to me is dead. His body is unrecognizable! I have my arm blown off. I certainly am in much better shape than my buddy, but that doesn't stop my pain. Nor does it stop me from wanting me to be whole; I want my arm back.

I think we need to examine the notion that no matter what level of trauma you endured, it is *all* a violation; it is *all* a boundary violation to the psyche, to the body, to the soul. Through this boundary violation, you ingested contaminants. You thought you were being given emotional nourishment but the emotional nourishment was tainted, just like you can have with contaminated water or a contaminated food. You drank a glass of water. It looked clear. It had no odor. It was so refreshing. Yet without you knowing it, you ingested a Parasite. This Parasite will make you feel horrible. It may take a considerable amount of time before you feel okay again. From time to time it may rear its ugly head and cause some distress. It's a horrible situation. You are not responsible for the pain you are experiencing. There is no need for guilt or shame. Feeling guilt and shame will only inhibit you from taking responsibility to get well. You need all of your physical, emotional, and spiritual energy to do all the necessary "treatment aspects" to flush this Parasite from your system.

So, what we need to do now is to examine the things that were said to you and done to you, and uncover how a child or a "younger you" may have interpreted those things. What I want you to do is to think about what kinds of experiences you did have and how your younger self might have interpreted or perceived those experiences. The key notion here is that if you ingested contaminants disguised as love, there is no responsibility on your part. No need for guilt. I can't tell you how to feel. I am just asking you to examine the innocence of the individual who unknowingly ingested contaminants. Unfortunately, many innocent people who are being abused and ingesting contaminants are stuck with the responsibility of working through the effects of that illness.

Perhaps you're saying to yourself, "This pain is too overwhelming." Indeed it well may be. However, to keep putting it on a shelf and suppressing it takes a terrible toll over time. Think about this: you have a pile of garbage in your attic and it's really not bothering anyone. You get some odor and maybe some bleed-through in the ceiling but it is tolerable. To go up in the attic and to actually weed through this garbage is terrifying. You might say, "Oh my God, I can never work through all of this." That is the Parasite talking. The longer it remains there, the worse the mess. I know you need to embrace the terror that you feel. The terror is a healthy, caution light, but it's a yellow light, not a red one. This is where the therapist is essential. With his or her help, you can take one step at a time, one day at a time. Don't do it alone! The caution light says, "Go slowly, go meticulously." Don't take it all on at once; recognize that you really have that kind of control.

Now, the Parasite will tell you that you don't have any control and attempt to overwhelm you. And that's how it reciprocally keeps itself within your system. "I am too big, too monstrous, and too horrible for you to deal with, so I'm just going to stay here and you're stuck with me." My simply saying that you do have control will not make you believe it today. Don't expect yourself to automatically connect and say, "Okay, I *do* have that kind of control." This is where the principles of the Twelve Step Program comes into play.

Step One: "I'm powerless with this. I have this thing in me that has directed my life. I don't like what it's doing. I can't trust people. I don't like me. I don't think I'm good enough." Whatever it's saying in there that keeps you the victim, you need to recognize that by yourself, you are powerless.

Step Two: "Coming to believe a Power greater than ourselves could restore us to sanity." Invoking a Higher Power to assist you in this is critical. You will, from time to time, seem overwhelmed with your feelings. That is a normal response to pain. It does feel overwhelming sometimes. Turning to a Higher Power to know that there is a presence of some goodness within you, assisting you in this struggle, is really critical. I will probably repeat the next statement several times. I need you to hear it over and over. I need you to believe the next statement. I've seen some very shrewd, intelligent, cunning, and powerful Parasites. I have *never* seen a Parasite stronger than the person and his or her Higher Power.

You might be saying to yourself, "That's hard to believe." Yes, it is. What makes it so hard to believe? "Because of the way it feels. It feels very powerful. The feelings that I have and the thoughts that I have are very powerful. They rule my life."

You're right! They *are* very powerful and for many people they have ruled their lives. That allows the Parasite to remain strong and the person, unfortunately, to remain victim. This affords the Parasite the power to trick you into victimizing yourself. Just the fact that it says to you "I am stronger than you....Hear me roar inside of you....Feel my wrath" is terrifying.

Do I want you to pretend that the Parasite is not powerful?

Absolutely not. It *is* powerful. It *is* cunning. But you are more powerful and with the help of your Higher Power you can overcome the power of the Parasite.

So, how do you start feeling this way? You hear what I am saying to you, but you can't tell me that you truly believe that yet. How can you be more powerful than this thing when it seems to have taken over your entire life?

The question you're asking is an excellent one. It's one that I have been asked by so many other people that it surely needs to be addressed here. However long you have worked at attempting to deal with this Parasite, you are not going to change this in a day. The Parasite has frightened you, terrorized you, caused you to victimize yourself, and played self-destructive games with you. Think about this. After the Parasite baits you to do something that you know is self-destructive, it turns around and says, "What's the matter with you? How could you do that? Look at how dumb you are." You can't win, or so it seems.

We need to examine the cyclical process and understand that, through this cyclical process, the Parasite gets its power and strength. It will take some time and some significant work, at first, to recognize when the Parasite is talking to you and corrupting you. Then, you need to believe that you are stronger than it is, with the help of your Higher Power. The Parasite wants you to be discouraged. It wants you to sit there and say, "There is no way in God's creation I can be stronger than this even with *three* Higher Powers." That's what you're probably sitting and thinking as you are reading this. You may say, "It doesn't sound like something else doing this; it sounds like me." It *is* you, at some level. However, in my view, it is you affected by this contaminant that is impacting how you think and how you feel, what you believe and how you behave. It's attached to those various parts of you: your thinking and your emotions. What it wants is the essence of who you are. It wants your soul.

About now, you might be feeling that this is getting really weird. Am I talking about an almost-demonic possession? Absolutely NOT! Cognitive psychology has for many, many years understood that we humans have internal monologues and dialogues. We all talk to ourselves inside our heads. Most of the time we are not even aware of the "chatter." But it is there. Sometimes it may feel like two parts talking to you, one saying, "Oh, what the hell, do it" and the other saying, "No, no, it is not right." This is an internal dialogue. Gestalt psychology relies very heavily on what is known as the "Parts Model." The theory essentially says that the psychological aspect of a human is likened to the physical. The body is composed of many parts and the parts work together to comprise a whole person. (The summaries of basic theoretical concepts included in this book are drawn from N. Murdock's excellent 2009 text, *Theories of Counseling and Psychotherapy*.) It is very important to appreciate that your psychological self also has many parts, each designed with specific tasks, just like the body parts.

Another useful idea is found in Adlerian theory, which proposes that early in childhood we learn many basic mistakes about ourselves and our world. These basic mistakes are what the

Parasite holds on to within our minds to keep us ill. A key basic mistake within the domain of abuse is, "You are damaged." Until you rectify that basic mistake at a feeling level, the Parasite holds on to the basic mistake. What do I mean? Well, I am sure, at some level, a part or parts of you knows you are not damaged, but you continue to feel damaged. You need to use your healthy parts to educate and, more importantly, convince those feeling parts that you are *not* damaged.

Sometimes the internal monologues are almost like old erroneous tapes that get played from time to time. When I was a young boy, my mother, who was and is terrified of illness, would tell me not to ever get my feet wet, because I would catch a cold. Growing up, I became fearful of getting my feet wet from the rain or snow. God forbid I should get my feet wet, catch a cold, and disappoint my mom! Now, I know, as an adult, that a cold is a virus and you don't catch a virus from getting your feet wet. Nevertheless, here I am, this adult male, ten years older than dirt, who still feels yucky inside when I get my feet wet. A genuine basic mistake that has not been rectified.

Theoretically, the Adlerian concept of basic mistakes holds true for all of us. Our task in adult life is to transform our big basic mistakes into smaller, less dysfunctional ones. Similarly, I believe all humans mature into adulthood with some type of Parasite. Many true parasites cause mild discomfort to the host. A physical example would be tapeworms. Other parasites, such as flatworms, can cause significant difficulties for the host. The ongoing battle with flatworms will require the host to seek medical intervention. Malaria, on the other hand, can be lethal. I believe the Parasites of the Adlerian basic mistakes are parallel to the biological para- sites. I also contend that the Parasite of abuse is one of the most deadly. I hope this clarifies how the infected part plays games in our minds. Sometimes, it may feel like a war inside your head. This war creates in you many different horrible feelings.

Let's stop here for a minute because, first of all, I think there is a battle going on. There is a disease in you, a Parasite, which exists for two reasons, as I've said before. One is to consume the host and the other, to replicate itself. And think about this. If you decide that this is not going to help, or worse yet, there is nothing that *can* help and you continue to victimize yourself, the Parasite has won. It will, eventually, destroy the host. The replication of itself, the pain, is the fallout from your unwillingness to recover. Those close to you, those who do care about you (even though it doesn't feel like they do all of the time) will be so negatively impacted that the Parasite will have replicated itself. That to me is a terrifying thought.

We need to be cautious. There is a battle going on inside. Many of my patients have likened it to a devil and an angel inside of them. I really don't think it's a matter of devils and angels. I think there are healthy and unhealthy parts inside the person, inside you. But sometimes the Parasite will play both sides. For example, at times you may have been very depressed. Say it's six o'clock in the morning, the alarm goes off and you have to get up and get ready for work. The Parasite then says to you, "Oh, God, I can't face another day, I feel terrible," and sometimes you even internalize that. "I can't get out of bed, I can't face today, I don't have the energy to take a shower." So you hit the snooze alarm and turn over. Next, another fifteen minutes goes by. The alarm goes off again. "Ohhhh, no way, I'm not going to work again." You get up and you call in sick. You go back to bed. And somehow you feel better. It's like, "There, this is better now, I don't have to face the day. I will get up later and shower and maybe I'll do something for myself." Perhaps you sleep until twelve o'clock, and you turn on the TV. You can't concentrate and before you know it it's five o'clock in the afternoon and you happen to pass a mirror in the bathroom or bedroom. Then, what you think is another part of you says: "Look at you, you're disgusting. Get a glimpse of yourself—you didn't even get out of bed today. What in God's name is wrong with you? You didn't even get in the shower. How could you be lovable? No wonder people don't like you." And then there is this commitment: "Well, tomorrow will be better." But tomorrow is not, and the cycle continues.

You may say, "Is that one of the good sides, one of the bad sides?" It is the various parts of you that the Parasite is playing against one another, baiting you into wasting your day and then crushing your spirit because you *did* waste your day. It's really important that you become aware of this cyclical aspect. Each time it cycles it builds momentum and momentum is power and that's why you feel so helpless sometimes because the Parasite has built up so much power. This is a struggle. This is a war.

You see, you are at war, but not with yourself. You are at war with your disease, the Parasite. You no longer need to feel like you must eliminate a part or parts of you that you believed caused the abuse. Many self-help books refer to healing the "inner child." For many victims, this healing the inner child is something very important. For you, it may be a necessary aspect of your healing. However, it is very difficult to do, especially when the Parasite has you convinced that your inner child is ultimately responsible for all your pain. I have heard so many patients tell me how they hate their "child part." They want to destroy that part. Again, this is where the Parasite gets its power. It logically tells you that since the child part caused all your pain, you will be pain-free when you eliminate it.

This is similar to the New Testament notion that "if your eye is the occasion of sin, pluck it out" (Mark 9:47). If it is your hand that is responsible for the sin, cut it off. In today's world, that would be self-mutilation. That type of self-mutilation would probably get you hospitalized. Is that really what you want to do? Do you really want to eliminate a vital part or parts of your psychological being? I believe, at least I hope, that your answer is: "No!" However, this is exactly what the Parasite has been baiting you to do. And the result has been self-defeating, self-debasing and self-abusive behaviors that have only continued your pain. You can place appropriate healthy boundaries on a part or parts of you. You can eliminate unwanted behaviors.

Now you can work at radiating these parts of you, in a sense, in order to shrink this Parasite from you. Here is where this approach becomes so different. The counseling I did prior to the development and use of this model of the Parasite was more like chemotherapy, which unfortunately kills off good cells as well as contaminated cells. I think this model is much more exact, much more direct. But nonetheless, like radiation, it can be a very painful process and never quick enough for you, because you are in pain. Nothing is ever quick enough. You're in pain and I wish we could stop your pain right now. What I can tell you, and I hope you can really hold on to this notion, is that we can begin to *shrink* your pain right now. It won't all stop, but I fully believe that you, with the help of your Higher Power, will attain this goal.

Now when I say, Higher Power, do I mean God? Is that who I am referring to? Well, for some people it *is* God. For some people it's the sun, for others Mother Earth. I borrow yet another aspect from the AA Twelve Step Program: whatever people choose to be their Higher Power *is* their Higher Power. I'm not talking religiosity. I'm talking spirituality, a connection with some other, if you would, "Being," that is beneficent and loving.

You may ask, "Well, why do I need a connection to another being to help me? Why can't I just dig inside by myself?" Well, for some people, if we're talking about a God, they might believe that there is a God that dwells within them. Whether it's a God who dwells within them, or the sun or Mother Earth outside of them, it is a concept of a power greater than themselves that they have connected with. A belief that there is a loving Being that is there with them, who cares about and loves them. A Being that does not want to see them in pain, and does not want them to be depressed. Your Power or Being knows you are in pain and depressed, and doesn't want to see you destroy yourself. A Power that knows your plight as well as you know it, and even better, because it is a Higher Power. We will need to talk about this Higher Power and how you imagine it again later.

What do I mean when I say that the Parasite wants to destroy you? Do I really mean that? Well, it wants to consume the host. If you look at it biologically, that's what a biologist would tell you. A parasite exists for two purposes: consume the host, and replicate itself.

Now, some people might think what I'm talking about is a little bizarre because I will allude to this Parasite as intelligent. I would also say this Parasite has "a mind of its own." For some that may be difficult to understand. It still is for me, at times.

Let us examine what we are told about various viruses and bacteria that we know exist as invaders of some other organism. Specifically, let's consider what we know about the Avian (bird) flu. We have been told that right now it is contained in certain birds and really poses no threat to humans. However, many scientists predict that in time it will find a way to invade a human organism. To me, that says that this parasite, or more specifically, this virus, does have some kind of "intelligence" or "a mind of its own." We know that some bacteria and some viruses have adjusted to many antibiotics that we use and developed resistances to them. So does an entity like this have a "mind of its own?" How is it doing this? I think to say that the Parasite in you has a "mind of its own" actually has some biological basis. This notion of "mind of its own" is simply a way for us humans to appreciate what it is doing so that we can counter its counter attacks.

So, if you stop minimizing the pain and you start realizing that you are powerful with the help of your Higher Power, will you immediately feel better? Unfortunately not. The Parasite will fight back, baiting you to fail, baiting you to lose hope. It won't just quietly leave its host. I think this is the point where the Higher Power, you, and your therapist must come together in a united battle front. You need to become aware and begin to recognize when the Parasite is attempting to play you. And remember—it plays hard.

Let me give you an example. I've been working with a young lady (let's call her Danielle) who has made tremendous progress in her war with the Parasite. A few months ago she came to me and said "I think I need to confront X." This would be an indirect level of confrontation with her abuser. She did not want to face the abuser personally, but rather wanted to confront someone in authority over the abuser. She really felt that this would help her minimize the Parasite's impact on her thoughts, her feelings and her subsequent behavior. She accomplished this confrontation. In fact, the person that she spoke with was very compassionate, very caring, very understanding, and believed her completely. I was present for that confrontation. This authority figure apologized on behalf of the abuser. And then all hell broke loose. Danielle started having incredible flashbacks to the traumatic event. She found herself driving past areas where the abuser lived, where the abuse occurred, and where the abuse accelerated. All this was to be expected, because the Parasite is powerful and cunning. I think with its "mind of its own" the Parasite said, "I have to throw everything I possibly can at her."

What is really helping Danielle now is recognizing that she simply needs to persist at what she has been doing and utilize some techniques like thought stoppage. (When a negative thought comes into your mind, yell "Stop! Cancel that thought! It isn't good for me." There's a lot of information about thought stoppage techniques in books and online.) Another turning point of her therapy was our recognition that she had never fully shared with anyone, including myself, the details of the abuse. We had talked around those details. This young lady really needed to discuss exactly what had happened during the abuse. As she began providing these details, we could see her getting healthier and healthier. However, here is where her Parasite showed that it has a "mind of its own." A few weeks later she said to me, "I think I need to confront the abuser directly." We were both aware of the serious pathological nature of this abuser. I said to her in a fair but firm manner, "You may need to do this for you. However, I cannot and will not go there with you. If you feel you really need to do this, I will respect your judgment. But in doing this, you will need to find another therapist because I see this as the Parasite baiting you into re-victimizing yourself. The abuser will never take responsibility. This person will turn around and blame you and you will reintegrate that responsibility—take it back onto yourself." That was one of the most difficult sessions we had had in two years.

Don't most therapists say that you should go back and confront the abuser? Some therapists do encourage this approach, although I look at it from the standpoint of "what good will it do?" Will it bring about healing, or will it bring about another level of abuse? I don't think you can simply prescribe to everyone the same treatment, because people are different. You may have the ego strength to stand up to your abuser and say "You lousy rotten person, do you have any clue of how much you hurt me?" Whether the person acknowledges that fact or not, you said it, and that may feel good for you. However, it may be disastrous if the abuser says, "I never did that. You seduced me. I was just loving you the way you told me you wanted to be loved." The Parasite will then absorb not only the pain, but the full responsibility for the pain.

Am I saying now that you should never confront the abuser? No. But I know that confronting the abuser is not the place to start. Nor do I believe all victims should confront their abusers. By the way, Danielle agreed a couple of weeks later that she actually felt relieved when I told her I would not go there with her. She has been doing well since.

Again you may ask, "So, therapists can tell me just how to get well?" One of the things I believe most firmly is that a person walks into my office with problems or issues in one hand, and solutions in the other. My job, and your therapist's job, is to believe in you and to believe that you have those answers. Then, we work at transferring that belief to you that you do indeed have the solutions. You and your therapist need to blow away the smoke or fog that clouds the issues and the solutions. Your therapist is going to need to look to you for some, if not all, of the answers you need. The clarity is not there yet, but the answers *are*. Some of them may need to be challenged—not to say you're wrong, but because sometimes the Parasite will contaminate a solution just as in the example of the young lady above who wanted to confront her abuser. The Parasite baited her into viewing this as a good solution, even though we knew the abuser would never take responsibility for the abuse. So when you ask, "What can I do?" the answer is this: you need to look inside yourself and discover your own personal solutions.

I would ask you to be very conscious of not allowing the Parasite to influence you or to speak for you in ascertaining what you need to heal. The Parasite is very good at baiting you into the "if only" game. One example of this is can be seen with a patient named "Chris." A professional woman in her late twenties, Chris was sexually abused by her mother's brother from age eight to thirteen. The uncle lived with her and her mother. Her father was deceased. I truly believe that it was Chris's plight that helped me conceive the Parasite model. I now know Chris's Parasite blatantly played the "if only" game: "If only I had someone to love me, I could believe that I was not damaged." I want you to examine this closely. Chris was convinced that she needed concrete proof in order to believe she wasn't damaged. She wanted the impossible. She wanted someone to love her, even though she refused to love herself. Our therapy focused on this single aspect for more than six months. Eventually, she grew more accepting of herself. She did, in time, find someone to love her and was married.

Approximately eight months later, she returned to therapy with another Parasitic "if only." This time, as you probably could guess, the "if only" was, "If only I could have a child, I would *really* know I'm not damaged."

It was at this point that I began to believe that abuse was a true disease. Her disease was raging. No matter what I could say or do, she was back to believing she was damaged, and this began to have a negative impact on her marriage. Intimacy with her husband, which initially had been positive, became cold and mechanical. She began to question his love. Therapy was not going anywhere and she was frustrated beyond belief. One day, in a session, her Parasite baited *me*. Unfortunately, I took the bait and said something that was hurtful. I immediately apologized, but the harm was done. She looked at me and said, "I am letting you down, and even you know I'm damaged." I felt completely sick inside. During the next few days, I consulted with my colleagues. I found myself saying, "This thing baited me, and I took the bait. This thing is smart, cunning, baffling, and powerful."

That is how I came to labeling the disease of abuse as a Parasite. The very next session, I continued to ask Chris to forgive my blunder. Fortunately, she did, and we began to rebuild our therapeutic relationship. Within a few weeks, I introduced Chris to the concept of the Parasite. Perhaps it was her trust in me, perhaps it was the weight of Chris's tremendous pain; regardless of what motivated her, the concept of the Parasite made perfect sense to her. Together, we set a new course for therapy. No longer would we attack the Parasite issue by issue which to me is analogous to chemotherapy. We began to identify the Parasite and direct therapy at radiating it, in order to force it to release its grip on the parts of Chris.

You might be asking, "What does he mean by that last statement?" Let me explain. Chris always kept a diary. I requested that she journal between sessions and bring this journal with her for us to review. In closely scrutinizing the journal, it became easy for us both to distinguish when the Parasite was "talking" and when Chris was talking. This helped her to begin to *talk back* to the parasite. There were times when the journal was "pure Chris," as we labeled it. She kept those entries in a separate folder. When she became aware of the Parasite talking in her head, she would go back and read the "pure Chris" folder. This became quite empowering for her, and she was able to definitely curtail the Parasitic thinking.

Eventually, Chris was able to embrace the fact that she was not damaged, and began to accept herself for who she is. She worked at the intimacy with her husband. She gave birth to a beautiful baby boy. Today, she would be the first to tell you that it wasn't giving birth that convinced her she was not damaged and not responsible for her abuse. By her own will, and with the help of her Higher Power, she convinced herself. When you attempt to ascertain what you need to heal yourself, remember Chris. Remember the answer lies in you!

"Will this Parasite ever be gone?" No. But it *can* be shrunk to a point where it no longer creates pain. That is what I mean by radiating it. And like many parasites, a significant portion of the Parasite is excreted out of your body. A part of it can lie dormant. It can surface its ugly head every now and then, but you will have new skills and the abilities to push it down. The key issue is that you need to maintain hope and a belief in a Power greater than yourself.

2

THE IMPACT OF ABUSE ON DEVELOPMENT

As previously stated, I, in collaboration with Dr. Andy Carey, had an article published in the American Counseling Association's *Journal of Counseling and Values.* The title of the article was "The Psycho-spiritual Dynamics of Adult Survivors." Although I believe most of what we theorized in the article remains true today, what was missing in the article were the concepts of the Parasite, the illness model, and the need to incorporate a Twelve Step Model of treatment into this mental health issue.

Dr. Carey who is now teaching at Shippensburg University left Marywood shortly after this article was published. We had not kept in touch until recently when we had a brief but powerful conversation. I believe we were both shocked by how our research has continued on parallel tracks. We contend that the main points contained in the article remain affirmed. Andy also concurs that there is a "thing" in those who were abused that, if not recognized, dooms treatment to failure.

Our original article concentrated on parent-child dynamics, with the parent as the abuser. Here, I have purposely used the term caretaker instead. This term was chosen to fit as many roles and functions of abusers as possible. Regardless of whether the abuser was a parent, an older sibling, an uncle, a neighbor, a teacher, a clergyman, or a coach, these people all had a function of caretaker. You trusted them to take care of you and they violated that trust. Rather than take care of you, they infected you with a horrible disease. Instead of taking care of you, they infected

you with a Parasite. I hope this chapter will give you some consolation. While it details a process of pain, it also demonstrates
the vitality, the strength and resilience of the human spirit to survive. Armed with the knowledge of what and how some issues
developed, and the knowledge of battling the Parasite and not
the self, you will survive.

The spiritual aspects of child development will not be presented in this chapter. In my continuing research, the notion of
Higher Power or God and the role the concept of Higher Power
or God plays in healing or non-healing has evolved to a most
significant level. Therefore, God as Healer, God as Persecutor
will be addressed in a separate chapter.

Ken Magid is a therapist who has examined and analyzed
"children without a conscience." He has observed severe inter-
ruptions in development in the first one and a half years of these
children's lives, and has hypothesized that these children suffer
from a complete lack of bonding. Identifying this lack of bonding offers much promise in treating troubled children. However,
Magid's theory does not account for those people who have
seemed to "survive" abuse, neglect and sexual assaults with a
highly functional and intact conscience, They have taken on the
role of the "good child." In this chapter, I am talking about individuals who exhibit the "good child" syndrome.

In research studies about survivors, three concepts appear over
and over again. The first is the attachment or bonding between
the survivor and his or her caretaker. The greater the problems
with bonding, the greater the dysfunction. People who have been
abused typically state that they desire no relationship with the
caretaker who abused them, but there is still a need and usually an
unconscious desire for a relationship. Emotional attachment with
caretakers is of utmost importance to children, especially when
they do not have strong attachment with others around them.

The second important component in the parent-child relationship is the desire for consistency. When caretakers are inconsis-

tent, children experience tremendous turmoil and anxiety. With dysfunctional, inconsistent caretakers/abusers, children become entangled in the emotions of love and rage while desperately seeking to balance them.

Children are unable to maintain two emotions simultaneously and therefore resort to the third concept, *splitting defenses*, which is well-known in the field of psychology. The concept of splitting enables children to maintain some semblance of equilibrium and a needed sense of attachment even though their caretakers are inconsistent or uncaring. The more dysfunctional the caretaker, the more children resort to extreme methods of remaining attached. They develop the notion that *they* are the problem. A contaminant, which is the Parasite, has infiltrated the child's sense of self, the ego, and begun to fragment it. This fragmentation, this splitting, appears to, for the moment, re-establish the child's equilibrium. This response allows children to internally maintain an idealized, all-loving view of their caretakers. This inner fantasy view of their caretakers enables children to maintain the needed caretaker attachment for security and safely. However, this inner safety and security with the caretaker is maintained at the expense of child's sense of self and self-worth. Children baited by the Parasite blame themselves for the "bad" that occurs in their lives. In addition, the longer the splitting occurs, the more the self-blame and destructive self-views are reinforced, and the more these patterns appear in relationships with others. The Parasite obtains its power from the repeating of this cycle again and again.

Faced with these inconsistencies, children continue to attempt to make logical and rational sense in an environment where no logic or reason exists. This is where the Parasite now takes over the child's ego by means of false internal statements that place the responsibility for the abuse on the child. The Parasite baits parts of the child's self to wage war with the parts that are responsible for the abuse. The need for attachment increases as the inconsistency grows. The terror, turmoil and pain created by the abuse itself, and the inconsistencies coupled with the need for attachment, create a dynamic and dramatic bonding process.

As this process continues, children baited by the Parasite internalize the source of their pain and create a dysfunctional bond with their caretakers. Children begin to formulate their own oppressive and controlling "critical parents." These critical parents evolve as internal representations of the children's external realities. The critical parents *within* the children form an allegiance with and develop a bond with the actual critical parents—the caretakers. This bond provides children with a basic sense of attachment, and develops some consistency in their otherwise inconsistent world. This negative bonding, produced by the Parasite, gives the Parasite increased power and control over the child's sense of self, as well as a continuing source of energy. The child will be infected with more and more contaminants of abusive, conditional "love." This provides the Parasite with an enormous and continual energy supply.

The noted psychologist Erik Erikson described a series of stages in a child's development. One stage involves developing a sense of trust. Dysfunctional bonding results in a basic sense of *mis*trust. Children can only "trust" that they will be hurt and that they deserve the hurt they experience. During the next Eriksonian stage, children influenced by the Parasite not only learn a sense of shame and doubt, but dramatically internalize these concepts. Children view themselves as the source of their caretaker's pain and therefore the cause or source of the abuse. Both children and abusers become even more bonded as they unite to "root out" the source of the abuse and pain. Children long for the moment that they will eventually, with the caretaker's assistance, be rid of the part of themselves that causes their pain, and afterwards achieve the intimacy they so desire.

The third year of life is recognized by several theorists as a critical year for children. Children should no longer need to split the mental representations of their caretakers into "good" and "bad" parents. According to Erikson, children must also master *initiative* over *guilt*. However, the abuse and the pain experienced by these children are far stronger than their initiative to achieve their goals. These children set as their goal a victory over the pain and terror they are experiencing. They attempt to end the abuse and inconsistency by "removing" or "exorcising" the cause of the pain within themselves. As the insurmountable battle wages, children continue to experience turmoil, pain, and terror. All initiatives aimed at disarming the "bad parent" are met with defeat. Children continually assume responsibility for their caretakers' moods and emotions. These children take the role of "pleaser" in order to reduce their caretaker's pain and displeasure.

As children continue to know only defeat in reducing their pain, they develop a deep sense of guilt. Erikson suggests that it is here that the most fateful split in the emotional self occurs, a split between potential human glory and potential self-destruction. Children, because of their guilt and failure to control caretaker behavior, give psychological birth to a fragmented self, committed to self-destruction. The Parasite makes certain that hostility remains aimed at the child's sense of self. The bond between caretaker and child is strengthened as these children now perpetuate their own destruction as the only means of staying attached to the external world where approval and love are at best conditional. Children imagine that there is a source of "evil" within themselves, and continually try to compensate for this evil. They attempt to regulate this evil by a commitment to self-punishment and/or self-destruction. This process allows the caretakers' critical parents and the children's critical parents to become entrenched as they unite to destroy the evil. This creates a greater sense of attachment for children to their caretakers. The fragmentation, the conviction of an evil existing within, and the guilt of being the cause of the pain for both the caretaker and themselves, forces these children to strive for perfection as compensation. However, as children aim for perfection, the paradoxical effect produces a tremendous sense of inferiority.

It is at this point in development that children's lives become a paradox. These children are often viewed by the outside world as model children. They are frequently praised outside the home and admired for their sense of responsibility and willingness to please, while inside the home they are criticized, battered, and sexually victimized. Their attempts to destroy the evil within, in actuality, destroy or suppress the free child almost totally.

These children are caught in a love/hate world, an endless double-bind. They hate the abuse, the intolerance, the pain, but feel they ultimately deserve these horrors. They hate and are terrorized by the sexual assaults, but long to be touched and held, perhaps, even in a pathological way, to be loved. They long for love and approval, but continue to feel unworthy of genuine love. They are victims of a negative self-fulfilling prophecy. They attempt to make logical, rational sense out of their pain and horror, but as they strive to make sense where none can be made, the Parasite reinforces the only logical explanation of their plight— that they deserve what is happening. They are not worthy of respect and allow themselves, as people pleasers, to be used as anyone desires. Often they believe they have no right to say *no* to anyone for any reason. From their perspective, their rage must be suppressed, not only because they deserve what is happening, but also because anger toward another is morally wrong. As they strive for perfection, they become increasingly aware of their imperfections. Morality and a sense of righteousness becomes another weapon in the Parasite's arsenal of self-destructive methods.

During adolescence these children typically become enmeshed in self-destructive behaviors. They may surface from their horror with an apparent diagnosis of a major mental illness, such as depression. As they emerge from adolescence into adulthood, they externally portray an excellent sense of goodness and model behavior. By over-identifying with "good" in hopes of eventually casting out the "evil" within, these teens survive the perils of adolescence.

As adults these individuals continue the self-abusive process. Many marry abusive spouses who allow them to remain united in a common bond with someone who will aid them in destroying the parts of the self responsible for their plight. Unaware of the Parasite that has infected them, they persist at expelling the truly innocent part or parts of them. There is, indeed, a "thing" in them that needs to be excreted. But what needs to be detached and excreted is the Parasite, not a healthy vital part of their ego.

Regardless of marital status or vocation, survivors remain psychologically isolated and self-absorbed. They are capable of giving love, but cannot receive love. They barricade parts of the self to protect other parts from evil. They as adults maintain self-destructive behaviors and in time, these behaviors surface as various mental disorders.

Before concluding this chapter, I believe it is essential that we take into account the age you were when you were abused. I know if Sally, a patient of mine whom you will meet later, were reading this chapter, she would say, "This doesn't pertain to me at all. I was eleven when the abuse occurred." You may be making the same or a similar statement. I have attempted to give a chronological order to the abuse. The research literature does tell us that most abuse begins early in a child's or infant's life. You may have been abused by a neighbor at age five, and therefore might too be saying with justification, "This does not pertain to me at all." I must be honest with you; there was a time when I wasn't sure. Soon after I began theorizing about the disease and specifically the Parasite, I questioned if the developmental theory was of any use to me and my patients. As I began introducing the Parasite to new patients, I began to realize that regardless of when the abuse began, or the type of abuse it was, the developmental difficulties were all the same. The only differences I could uncover were differences in *degree* of difficulties. I suggest that no matter what type of abuse is experienced or at what age the abuse occurs, the trauma of abuse has the same results. Perhaps this is because the ego in childhood and adolescence is not fully developed and is therefore somewhat fragile. Perhaps because of the Parasite's ability to fragment the self, developmental issues such as trust which had previously been resolved, become unresolved. I can only hypothesize. I can only tell you that the answer to that question is beyond the scope of this book.

3

SOME ISSUES TO CONSIDER TO AID YOU IN THERAPY

Semantics or Genuine Thought Patterns

Over the past twenty-five years, I have come to see vividly how the words we use shape our thought patterns. Take the word *deserve*. "I deserve a better job." "I deserve respect." I believe deserve is a "bad word." If said enough, people begin to believe they are entitled. Sure, you may *need* a better job, or certainly *need* respect, but what are you doing to get a better job, or earn respect? If you just go through life saying "I deserve" and don't work to acquire what you need, you are just going to become an angry person.

I have a wonderful wife, and we have two great adult children. Do we deserve them? In comparison to other families, have we done something special? I think not! Have I done something so terrible that I deserve to lose them? I hope not! Babies are born addicted to the drugs their mothers ingested during their pregnancy. Do you think they "deserve" to come into this world addicted? Talented, gifted people like athletes make millions of dollars playing games. Do you think they "deserve" that? Did you deserve to be abused?

People have issues, situations in their lives—some good, some horrible. Rather than getting stuck in the "I do deserve" or "I don't deserve," suppose we simply work at coping. Coping with the negative things in our life and working at minimizing the pain from them. A twelve-steps slogan is KISS—Keep It Simple,

Stupid. We need to keep life as simple as possible. We need to accept life on life's terms.

Another horrible word is *worthy*. As human beings, are we always worthy of having someone love us? Does any child need to be worthy of safety from abuse? Suppose we simply say to ourselves that these concepts—deserving, worthy, justice, etc. don't always exist in this world. Maybe they do in an afterlife, but I really don't see them reliably present in this world.

Albert Ellis, in his counseling theory, believed that there are other "bad" words that are problematic. The "shoulda, coulda, wouldas" are among these problematic words. "I should never have trusted him." How were you supposed to know? Where is it written that you should never trust a person who appears to be trustworthy? Where is it written that you should never trust a father, a neighbor, a teacher, a coach, a clergyperson? These words lead to unrealistic expectations for ourselves. "I should always please my significant other." Really? That's impossible! Ellis would say "Don't 'should' on yourself." I believe he has a point.

Another "bad" word for me is *try*. To me, trying implies failure. I have a problem when my students or my patients tell me that they will try to do whatever. I prefer the phrase "work at" instead. "I will work at learning this new concept." "I will work at excreting the Parasite." The phrase "work at," to me, implies more commitment. It also allows for more success. Right now I am working at writing this book. It is far from complete. It is far from a best-seller. But, I am working at it, and every day that I work at it, I am one step closer to my goal.

You may ask, "Where is he going with this? Why is he focused on semantics?" Because I believe that the Parasite will use many of these words (and others) to play its game in your head and heart. We need to be cognizant of the words and the subsequent games that the Parasite plays. Again, we need to listen to the chatter in our heads and work at becoming more rational about our expectations of the self and others.

You Have a Choice, and There is Power in That Choice

I am sure that you want to be rid of the pain and turmoil that you are in right now. But, at the same time, you don't want to experience the newer, unfamiliar type of pain involved in identifying, radiating and excreting the Parasite. Can you work at committing all of you, all of your psychological and spiritual resources to not allowing the Parasite to consume any more of your life? You may be thinking that you don't have a choice. I believe that you *do* have a choice and there is power in that choice. You see, right now the Parasite is playing you. It will tell you that you have to get rid of it. It will attempt to bait you into a war with it, as it tells you that you can't win the war. Nothing and no one can force you to work at eliminating the Parasite. You may say, "But the other choice is to allow all this pain to continue and for me to remain miserable." That is true. But you still have a choice. Alcoholics and drug addicts have a choice. They can continue to use, or they can or work at recovering. They have a choice, and so do you!

Choosing the road to recovering can be and is empowering. Facing the Parasite and committing to take back its power because you need to—that is very empowering. There is an incredible paradox here. In a New Testament quote that I personally love, St. Paul says, "My grace is sufficient for you, for power is perfected in weakness." Power is perfected in weakness! In other words, admitting you are weak, admitting you are powerless without a Higher Power, and seeing that you do have a choice will be very empowering for you. Take that power and hold on to it.

Altering Perceptions

Psychology tells us that there is a reciprocal process between our cognition (thoughts) and affect (emotions.) If I think about my dad who passed a few years ago, I may feel very sad. As I continue to experience this sad feeling, I may begin to think about the horrible disease that reduced a man who was bigger than life to a child who didn't know me. Each cycle of thoughts and feelings, feelings and thoughts, establishes momentum. Given a few moments in this cycle, you begin to feel like your head is spinning. Yet, when I look at his picture, and I remember his goodness, I begin to feel gratitude for having him as a dad. However, when I think of our neighbor, a whole gamut of feelings arises almost instantaneously. Perhaps we need not go there, but I think you get the picture.

Our personal history and our perception of that history tend to color our view of the world. If your history taught you that you were damaged, you will perceive yourself as damaged, no matter how good you may look or feel today. However, perceptions can be altered. You can learn and process new and more accurate information. Nonetheless, you must be willing to make the necessary adjustment in your perception.

Let me give you another example. We are on a bus trip to New York City. It is a cloudy, dreary February day. As the bus traverses through the streets of Manhattan, we see hordes of people. The streets are somewhat dirty. Everybody looks either very busy or very unhappy. We get dropped off at the Empire State Building. We decide to walk up ten flights of steps. When we reach the tenth floor, we look out a window. Now, the city begins to look quite different. It is the same city, but our perception of it has been altered by our different view. Suddenly, it is nicer, cleaner, and less congested. We then decide to climb up to the observation deck. It is a long, hard, almost exhausting walk, but, we get there. When we look out once more at the same city, it now looks totally different. Three different views of the same city. All are real, but all are different and our perception of Manhattan has been altered. (For the sake of this analogy, humor me. There *are* elevators at the Empire State Building!)

I believe what you need to do in counseling is somewhat similar to the above example. If you truly desire to alter your perception of yourself, you can and you will. When you alter the perception of yourself, you will begin to think and feel differently. But in order to accomplish this you must climb the stairs. There are no elevators. The climb will be difficult and sometimes exhausting, but when you reach the floor you need to be on, the climb will be more than worth it. When you realize that you are not damaged, not broken, and not responsible for your abuse, you will stop the self-abasing statements and give yourself the respect you need. Then you will know the climb was worth it.

You might be thinking, "That sounds great, but I will never get there." I ask you to answer this question: Is that you or the Parasite? Your response might very well be, "How the hell should I know? It feels like me, but you keep saying it's the Parasite. I have been feeling like this all my life. Now you're telling me that I need to distinguish what is me and what is the Parasite. I don't know what is me! If that's not me, who am I? I don't really know *who* I am!"

All of your fears are most legitimate. Start by validating your right to be confused and fearful, and embrace those feelings. They are normal. Actually, they are quite healthy. Anytime a person begins in therapy, it can be very terrifying, regardless of the issue. "Will I be successful? What will the outcome be? Will I become someone I don't want to be? Will I uncover some deep, dark secret about me? Will therapy turn me into a chicken?" (Just kidding about that one.) All of these are legitimate questions and result in legitimate fears. Don't allow the Parasite to use your thoughts and questions to prevent you from engaging in therapy. Fear of the unknown is normal. Therapy is frightening. Sometimes, therapy can be hurtful. A competent, ethical therapist will tell you that sometimes therapy can be harmful. Embrace your fear! Remember the yellow light and proceed cautiously.

I have a dream of someday being able to jump into a swimming pool off the high board. Yes, even old men can have dreams! So

I began taking swimming lessons, because I am terrified of deep water. I go around to the shallow end and test the water. Then I get in slowly. I think there is another metaphor here for you. I know you want to dive into therapy off the high board, but you are frightened. Come around with me to the shallow end and wade into the water. It is much less frightening and just as effective at getting you into the pool.

Now, let me respond to your second point of knowing when the Parasite is talking to you, and when you are talking to you. It is a learning process of listening closely to your internal monologues and dialogues. The closer you listen, the more you will recognize if it is you or the Parasite. It is definitely a process of trial and error. There are times you will succumb to the Parasite. It is critical to understand that you can't win every battle. Be patient and forgiving of yourself when you lose one. The Parasite hates that. You can't win every battle. You only need to win the war. That's what's critical.

Feelings: Real to You, But Are They Objective Reality?

You may sit there as an adult person and tell me that you feel like a crummy little kid. That certainly is real to you. You have a right to those feelings. Those feelings must be validated. But it doesn't mean that those feelings are an external reality. I don't see a crummy kid, I don't see a little kid. If I gave you a mirror, and asked if you saw a crummy little kid, I'm sure you would have to say, "I see an adult." This is the reality.

The feelings don't go away, and I respect that. They are not supposed to go away, but they can be altered if you choose to alter them. Again, it's your choice. Do you choose to alter them? Do you choose to see this adult, or do you want to continue to see a crummy little kid? If you don't want to see a crummy little kid then begin to work at seeing something different. Feelings are real to the person, and they identify where the person is emotionally at a given moment in time. But they do not necessarily involve external reality. If you said to me "I feel like a piece of garbage," I'm not going to put you in a plastic bag and put you on the stoop for the garbage man. If you said to me, "John, I feel so good today I could fly," I'm not letting you go out that fourth story window. But those feelings, positive and negative, could very much be your reality at that given moment. You feel like garbage today or you feel so good that, wow, you could fly. They are internal realities, but they are not an external reality. And that's what we need to work on. What's the external reality?

No feelings are bad. There are positive and negative feelings. The positive ones precipitate a good overall mood when we're experiencing them. Examples of positive feelings are love and happiness and laughter and excitement and anticipation. And there are the negative ones that, when we are experiencing them, can be distressing; they can be downers and they can be painful. Grief, guilt, depression, things you know too well. They don't necessarily define you. You can *feel* like a crummy little kid, but that does not mean that you *are* a crummy little kid.

Think about this. If I were attempting to control you and make you feel bad about yourself, would I put forth an image of an attractive, intelligent, competent person—or this crummy little kid? I think you get the point.

What you have never done, but need to do, is to love the crummy little kid as much as you would love this intelligent, attractive adult. Attack the Parasite! Drive *it* out of you. Don't attempt to drive the child part out of you. The child is innocent and an essential part of who you are. Picture two children, identical twins, approximately two years old. One of them has just had a bath, and his mother has sprinkled him with baby powder. He smells precious and he looks precious—giggling and cuddly. Now, I would doubt you would have any difficulty picking up and just cuddling this little child. Correct? Now, picture the twin with a terrible cold. The child has (excuse me) a snotty nose and some of the mucus is crusted on the back of her hair. She has poop in her pants and up her back. She is feeling kind of miserable and whiny. Now, I doubt you want to pick up and cuddle *this* child. My challenge to you? See how much she needs the cuddling, she needs the love! Your crummy little child needs it. And maybe when you start cuddling your crummy little kid part of you, you will see that that child is really pristine, smelling of baby powder and cooing to someone who loves her. Someone sees her beauty. Most importantly, someone sees her innocence. You see, the child *is* beautiful. She is an important part of you. It was only the Parasite who made her look and feel bad. It was the Parasite who told you to get rid of her so you could feel good again. The Parasite is saying, "She got you into this. Get rid of her." When you stop listening to the Parasite, and work at integrating this child part and other parts of you, you are radiating the Parasite.

Didn't I Have A Right to a Happy Childhood?

Over the last twenty-five years, many (if not all) of my patients have said to me that they believed they deserved a happy childhood. (See, there's that bad word again!) If they don't use the word "deserved," they may use the phrase "right to." Or they might say they "should have" had a happy childhood. I believe this is where the Parasite really gets its power. "You deserved a happy childhood, and you didn't get it. So sit here and be miserable for the rest of your life. You got screwed. You are damaged." As I have said in the developmental section, the child is attempting to make sense of this horribly painful non-sense. The Parasite will then work on the parts of the self to ensure fragmentation. In this way, the Parasite keeps you at war with yourself. The Parasite may have baited you to be at war with life itself. You may have given up on hopes and dreams, because there seems to be no use. Life just won't let you win. The Parasite may have also baited you into being at war with God. "God allowed this to happen. God could have stopped it." What might even be worse of all, is that God picked this to happen to you. "God is a real SOB." And, all this time you have been at war with yourself, life, and/ or God, the Parasite has been getting stronger and you weaker.

What I am about to say in this section is one of the most difficult concepts in this text. I believe that holding onto the notion that you had the right to a happy childhood is how the Parasite keeps you a victim. No matter what words we use—deserve, right, guarantee or expectation—I believe all are problematic. They are words that keep you from moving on with your life. I wish every child had a happy childhood, but you know all too well that that is not the reality. There is nothing I can say or do to make it up to you. There is nothing you can say or do to get your childhood back. But there is something you can do today to begin to take the power back from the Parasite. There is something that you can do today to stop victimizing yourself, and work at becoming a survivor. There is something you can do to make sure the Parasite does not take one more minute of your life: Stop just existing and waiting for something to fix you. You are NOT broken!

Did I Lose My Innocence?

I think we can take a lot of things away from a child. I think we can take away childhood. I think we can destroy it. But I don't think we can ever take their innocence.

Many of my patients say that their innocence was taken away from them. I know that it feels like that to them, but I don't really believe that abuse takes away a child's innocence. That's part of the problem. The Parasite is telling the person who has been abused that her innocence, her virginity, her purity have been taken away. That's not true. The abuser took the childhood, portions of it or all of it. However, no abuse can truly take away the innocence or purity of a child.

Many of the religions in today's world have what are believed to be holy artifacts: a book, a symbol, blessed water, or bread. In Catholicism, people believe that a consecrated piece of bread is the body of Christ. For Catholics, it is the Holy of Holies. Suppose an evil person took a consecrated Host and desecrated it. Through that desecration, did that person destroy the holiness of the Host? Did that person take away its innocence or its purity? I think not! He violated it! That is true. He perhaps altered the Host's outward appearance. However, the internal form remains unharmed.

In a similar fashion, you may have experienced some physical scarring in your genital area. However, your true internal form remains unharmed. It is the Parasite that wants you to believe that you are damaged. You are not! You have been violated, but you have not lost your innocence. You need to believe this and take the power back from the abuser. The abuser and the pain of the abuse took your hope of a happy childhood. Do not let the abuser take anything else. Hold onto the notion that your innocence, your purity is still inside of you. You need to love that part of you that you perceive as a crummy little kid. She may look dirty. She may seem disheveled. She may be really angry. However, when you truly embrace her, you will perceive that she is innocent. She is not damaged.

So How Do I Explain Dysfunctional Parenting?

I am not sure I really can explain dysfunctional parenting. I don't want to believe any parent would bring a child into this world just to abuse the child. I know there are some very sick, perhaps evil people out there. However, I want to believe that most parents bring children into this world with the best of intentions. As they say, though, the road to hell is paved with good intentions. Good intentions are not sufficient to produce good parenting. We recognize that no parent is perfect. The reality is that some parents are better than others. Some parents are sick. Some participate in evil. Some just plain *suck* as parents. I truly regret this reality. Perhaps a metaphor that I use will help us better understand such poor or bad parenting.

Imagine parenting to be like an amphibious landing on a hostile beach. It is D-Day, when the Allies launched an assault on the Normandy coast. You see these landing crafts (the parents) coming from the Mother Ship and on the landing craft are the troops (children). Each landing craft wants to get its troops safely onto the beach. They hover around the Mother Ship and eventually they are given the signal to go off. As they approach the beach (which in reality is adulthood), obstacles get in their way—life obstacles. Some, perhaps are simply the evils that just exist in the world from unforeseen circumstances. If I were born with a cleft palate, is that just a random obstacle? If I were born with Down Syndrome, would there be any rhyme or reason for this? Genetically, we can explain it. But why does a mother give birth to one Down Syndrome child and subsequently two normal, healthy children?

So (back to our metaphor), as these landing craft, these parents attempt to get their children onto the beach safely, into adulthood safely, some things go awry. Some landing craft get blown up before they even get close to the beach. Those kids didn't stand a chance. An example of this would be the mother who wouldn't give up her cocaine addiction and left her prenatal infant riddled with all kinds of brain damage. It's what we call life— the role of the dice. It's unfair. It's not systematic. There is no rhyme or reason. It happens. I don't know that we feeble humans can ever sit here and make sense out of it, but we keep attempting to. Some troops get dropped off a half-mile off shore with all their equipment (their baggage) weighing them down. They struggle mightily, and as they get their heads above water, they see some landing craft get right onto the beach, delivering some other troops. Not a scratch, not even wet. I'm sure they say, "Son of a bitch, why me? Why wasn't I that lucky?" And I would say to them, "I don't know." But I do know this: Wherever you were dropped off, with whatever obstacles you encounter as you approach adulthood, that's where your war starts. And if you don't start battling back right there you are going to drown. You are going to get killed. You don't stand a chance. Your war started somewhere off-shore. During the last number of years you've been swimming to get to the beach. As a victim, your war started wherever you were dropped off. You're limping, you're wounded, but you're not damaged, and that's a key difference. The Parasite will tell you that you are damaged. It will tell you that you were marked from the minute you left the Mother Ship. You were marked with a big D on your forehead. You are damaged goods.

This is one of the key negative notions you need to dispel; you are not damaged goods. No one took your innocence; no one took your purity. They can violate your body but they did not violate your soul. The soul is where your innocence is; the soul is where your purity is. The soul is where your virginity prevails. The Parasite wants the soul, and can penetrate it by scratching away and slowly destroying that essence of who you are. Once you are no longer you, it will take your pain and bait you to abuse yourself continuously, and/or abuse those around you. It baits you into actively seeking something that no one can give you, your childhood. We can't give that back to you. You asked me what you need to do to heal. One of the critical things you need to do is grieve your childhood, because no one can give that back to you.

Grieving The Loss of Your Childhood

Grieve your childhood. The Parasite will tell you that you can get it back. It will also tell you some way to get it back. No matter what the Parasite tells you, though, you cannot get it back. It's not going to come back. You can't be a five-year-old again. You can't, in a sense, go back to the Mother Ship and then come back to shore. So your childhood needs to be mourned. But in your grief, there is the hope that no one can take another minute of your life because now you're the adult trooper. You're on shore, and you're on your feet.

You may have spent a lot of time moaning about your childhood, but perhaps not really grieving this childhood. Do you hear the difference between what you have been doing and what I'm saying? What I'm saying is to work at accepting the loss. Some people may have said to you, "Get over it. Stop moaning. Get on with your life." Is that what I am saying? Definitely not! I have no idea what "Get over it" even means. It's a stupid phrase. And I am not saying, "Stop moaning about it." You and I may moan about some things that happened to us for the rest of our lives. I don't know if you could ever "get over" your abuse. But I think you *can* work through the abuse.

There have been things in my life that have happened to me. Some wonderful, some good, and some not-so-good things that I will carry to my grave. Take the loss of one's parents. Do you ever get over that? For those who have lost a child: do they ever get over that? Think about those who have lost limbs or families or careers to drugs and alcohol. Are they going to get over that? You can commit to working through it and there is a definite hope that you can work through it. I don't know that it gets better, but I do know it gets easier. Even though some things may not get better, it truly does get easier to cope because you're working through it. But you must continuously cope. So, am I saying that by grieving the loss of your childhood, you will completely accept this loss? I think you work toward some level of acceptance. If you examine the stages of grief and bereavement (denial, anger, bargaining, depression, acceptance) they are not solid steps, they are stages. You can't expect to just do the five steps and arrive at acceptance and stay there always. You don't just arrive. You work at a level of acceptance. That's as good as it gets. And today I can accept some things better than I did yesterday. Tomorrow I might not accept anything. It fluctuates. Again, though, I think when you have a sense of goodness about yourself it becomes easier to accept the fluctuations. Go back to the developmental aspects that you've read about in chapter two. Remember the notion of perfectionism and people-pleasing. You're a perfectionist, and you will want to do this perfectly. That, unfortunately, is not possible for us. We are merely human.

The Hunt For The Evil

I have worked with clients during their course of treatment for several years, meeting once a week or every two weeks. As they begin to make progress, the Parasite baits them into playing a game with themselves and with me. This revolves around the core belief or "Basic Mistake" that there is something inherently bad in them that caused the abuse. The game might be called "Can you top this?" or "Wait until you discover this about me." For example, I was working with a young lady who could not bear to look at the picture of my adult children that I have displayed in my office. I couldn't for the longest time appreciate why she would twist her body in a particular position on the couch. It looked to be a terribly uncomfortable position. After weeks of wondering, she made a comment about how terrible I was going to think she was. Of course I asked her what she meant by that statement. She said, "I'm just a terrible person, you don't know."

It probably took us two or three more sessions for her to tell me that she couldn't look at the picture of my adult children because she felt jealous of them. She was convinced that I would think she was horrible if I knew how jealous of my children she was. She admitted she really didn't like my children, even though she had never met them. But she saw me as a caring father. *She* wanted a caring father, not the biological father who sexually abused her. I felt this was a completely natural response. Why would you not be jealous of something that someone else has?

I realize that, in some denominations, some religions, jealousy may be seen as a sin, a violation of God's rules. Jealousy and envy are similar. A certain amount of envy or jealousy is quite normal. What I call destructive envy, on the other hand, is more behavioral and can be viewed as aberrant. I think if you have a beautiful, brand-new black Mercedes, with gray leather interior, I might be quite envious of you and your car. I think that is normal. If I am very hungry and I saw you eating a delicious, delectable bacon cheeseburger, I might be a little envious of that, especially if I don't have a buck in my pocket to buy that delectable cheeseburger. I think that's normal human behavior, too. Destructive envy, on the other hand, is where I take it to a point that if I can't have it, you can't either. So I destroy your new car. I take the hamburger away from you and either eat it or throw it away but do not let you have it. I think that's where we transgress against humanity and maybe even against God's laws. So back to the title of this section—The Hunt for the Evil. The Hunt for the Evil is the Parasite saying, "If they only knew this about me, they couldn't possibly respect me."

This Hunt for the Evil is a process we need to examine in detail. I also believe it is a mechanism by which persons may uncover some deep-rooted aspects of themselves. Obviously the Parasite has convinced you that you are damaged goods and you are responsible for what happened. We've already talked about the child's desire to make sense out of non-sense. The child attempts to make some logical sense out of the horror of abuse. Of course, it *doesn't* make sense. You may look for something within the core of you as being inherently bad or evil. If and when you find it, you can then explain the abuse. When you find it, then the abuse will make sense. But believe me, it will *never* make sense. You may need to do this: you may need to play the "wait till you hear this about me" game. It may help you reveal the horrible things that happened to you. You and your therapist need to understand that there is a process that you need to go through. It's not just about you revealing some bad things about you or that happened to you. Perhaps one of the most poignant issues is when a person says "I wanted him to touch me; I wanted to feel special, and I needed to be loved." This is a core fear for many victims, that perhaps they invited the abuse. It's normal for us to want to be touched, to be loved, to be held. I have never heard a victim say "I wanted to be touched like that, there." In fact, it's the reverse. "I wanted to be touched, but not there, not like that." Perhaps you wanted certain things from the abuser or you enjoyed being special to the abuser during the time you were being abused. Or perhaps you even felt some arousal in the genitalia. This is biologically normal. It does not make the abuse your fault.

When we think about this, we need to appreciate what normal human functioning is. Is it normal for a four- or five-year-old little boy to be touching his genitals? Of course. Is it normal for a little girl? Believe it or not, it is. You know what? It feels good. I do not think, contrary to Freud's notion, that children are really getting what we think of as sexual pleasure. The children *are* getting pleasure. Do they know that they are masturbating? Absolutely not! But again, you need to understand the fact that the body is responding as it's programmed to respond. Even at an older age, if a woman's body is being touched against her will, the body still might respond with some sensations, some automatic lubrication, etc. This needs to be understood. The body is responding. The body doesn't know it's being abused. The mind does.

As a child or an adolescent victim of abuse, you were most likely saying, "This is wrong. This shouldn't be happening." And you were right. But your body might have been saying, "This feels good." Did you enjoy it? Did you do something to cause it? No, you did not! You did not enjoy being abused! You may have enjoyed some of the aspects of feeling close to someone. The Parasite will play on your confusion, and will convince you that you are inherently evil. In this process, you and your therapist come together and examine in detail all aspects of the abuse. This provides you with an opportunity to flush those aspects out. The doubts you may have about being responsible are typically where you believe the evil lies.

You may also think that some other feelings are an indication of the evil: "I feel jealous toward my therapist's children. I feel love toward my therapist because the therapist is the first person who ever gave me undivided positive attention without asking for anything." You may have very strong feelings toward your therapist, maybe even sexual feelings. Given the nature of the therapeutic process, these feelings can often occur, and it is considered quite normal. These feelings are not an indicator of evil. Of course, it is unethical for both patient and therapist to act on these feelings, because the therapist is duty-bound to protect you in your vulnerability. However, these feelings, positive or negative, are simply an indicator of your humanity.

These aspects need to be explored in order for you to be convinced that there is no evil in you.   However, at some point in time during the therapy process, there needs to be a halt to the Hunt for the Evil. After a considerable amount of time, I directly ask my patients if they are convinced there is no evil in them. Many times I simply present this concept: "You are a bright, articulate and insightful person who has lived in your body for all these years and you have not found any evil. And do you know why that is?" Always the response from my patients is, "Because there isn't any." Exactly! Both you and your therapist have not found any evil because it is not there. The Parasite wants you to keep hunting for the evil; this is how it maintains its grip on you. I know people who come into my office who have been abusers themselves. Some other patients have done terrible things to other people, sometimes to their spouses. These patients have violated the boundaries of others. They know exactly what they have done, and it's at the forefront of their minds. We don't have to hunt for it. I'm not completely certain they are inherently evil. However, as you know too well, we humans are capable of doing truly evil things.

Another aspect in this Hunt for the Evil is the necessity to go back and actually give details of the abuse. Often, the Parasite holds some details as evidence of the evil. You and your therapist need to be aware of the fact that, together, you have to do a detailed examination of the abuse beyond simply stating that you were abused and it was a horror. From your standpoint, you or the Parasite might say, "I was abused, but you don't know that I put his penis in my mouth. You know I was abused but you don't know that I let her shove some kind of object into my vagina and into my anus. I said nothing. I froze. I could have screamed. I didn't. I must be evil." None of these things make you evil. I know you need enough time to deal with each detail, but at some point in time you need to finally cease the Hunt for the Evil with the firm belief that there is no evil in you to be found.

Visiting The Ovens

This next section is very closely related to the Hunt for the Evil. Most, if not all of my patients, have demonstrated a need to go back to the scene of their abuse. I have come to believe that this is critical to the success of the therapeutic process. You, during your abuse, may have experienced a psychological disconnect from yourself. Many victims report a dissociative type of experience, wherein a part or parts of them seem to leave their body. They report being able to know what was happening to them, but not being able to have any feelings about what was happening. This is quite normal in any trauma. The horrible pain of the event causes you to "shut down." Perhaps an example would help. Think of a circuit breaker within an electrical panel box. If you put too much strain on a particular electrical line, the circuit breaker in the panel box trips, shutting down the power to that line. The breaker trips the line to prevent a disaster. If the breaker didn't trip, the line would overheat and cause an electrical fire. Clearly, the tripping of the breaker is a positive thing, because it prevented a disaster. In a similar fashion, defense mechanisms in humans trip in order to prevent a psychological disaster. So if you disconnected from yourself during the abuse, or you have difficulty knowing what you felt, you are not alone. Given the circumstances of the trauma, your defenses tripped to protect you. Although you may feel it is problematic (and it is), you are still very normal.

What is problematic is the fact that you may need to revisit the abuse in order to reconnect with those parts of you that tripped. You may need to reconnect with your feelings that became isolated. While this is not pleasant, it can be most helpful.

There are other reasons why you may need to revisit the abuse. I believe the most important reason is for you to receive validation. Yes, this thing did happen. Yes, it was horrible. I can't even imagine what the pain must have been like. Usually, this need for validation is not a one-time event. So, you may need to go back numerous times.

If I may, I would like to use an analogy. During the Holocaust, millions of people suffered horrible, evil atrocities. The kind of torture and suffering they experienced is incomprehensible. But those atrocities really happened. The survivors of the camps need the people of the world to validate that this indeed did happen. They need us to bear witness to the crimes committed against them. They need us to commit to never allowing this to happen again. There is nothing that we can do to make it up to them. What is done, is done. No human can fix it.

In a similar way, you may need this type of validation. Validation to affirm that this, indeed, was a personal atrocity. Validation that the violation you experienced was horrible. Validation of the fact that no child should ever be abused. Validation of how incomprehensible it is that any child could be exposed to that kind of pain. Validation of the fact that we know we can't make it all better. We can only help you heal the pain that you did nothing to cause. However, while revisiting the abuse can be most helpful to the healing process, the Parasite can also manipulate you into re-abusing yourself. The concern here is that when you revisit the camp (the abuse scene), the Parasite can bait you into getting back into the oven or the gas chamber and harm yourself further. As a therapist, I have witnessed this all too often. You and your therapist must be clear on the purpose and the goal of revisiting the abuse. You need to call forth all the parts of you to answer the questions: What good will it do? What do I hope to gain? What need do I hope to fulfill from this revisiting?

At this point in my understanding of the abuse cycle and the Parasite, I remain most willing to walk with my patients through the horrors of the camp. However, before we go there, I freely ask them to clarify the purpose of the revisiting. I also bluntly say, "If this will do you some good, I will go to hell and back with you. However, if you are going back simply to get in the oven or the gas chamber to re-abuse yourself, I cannot and will not go with you. While I can't undo the abuse you experienced, I can work at making sure I am not a part of your re-abuse." When patients hear this for the first time, they are surprised and shocked. However, after some intense discussion, they become aware of the necessity of using the yellow light and proceeding cautiously.

4

VICTIM VS. SURVIVOR:
BECOMING A SURVIVOR

You may have noticed that I have repeatedly used the term *victim* and not *survivor*. Perhaps this has even made you quite uncomfortable. I hope I have not caused you discomfort. However, the choice of the term victim is purposeful. As I have already stated, the Parasite of abuse creates a cycle of self-abuse. You do things that you hope will make you feel better, only to discover that afterwards you feel worse. You may drink tonight to dull the pain, and then awaken tomorrow feeling worse. Do you think this is self-abusive? You bought a cheesecake for dessert last night for a special someone. He had to cancel. It seems that is always the way things happen. You eat half of it. You're angry. You're hurt. The cheesecake makes you feel good. The next morning you get on the scale. You are up two more pounds. That is ten pounds in the past month. You go to work, then literally beat yourself up at the gym. Afterwards, you go home and consume the other half of the cheesecake. Do you think this is self-abusive?

Another example: You are a woman of high moral character. You have made a commitment to yourself not to have sex with just anyone, because you only feel dirty afterwards. However, you are feeling so empty, and so alone. The pain is terrible. You go out with a friend for a drink. A guy asks you to dance. Afterwards, you sit and talk for a while. He seems nice, and he is pretty good looking. He wants to hold you. He thinks you're nice. Before you know it, it is over. Wham! Bam! Thank you ma'am! And you thought you felt horrible *before* you went out. Now, you feel cheap, dirty, used and disgusting. Do you think this is self-abusive?

You may not go to these lengths with self-abuse. Many times, victims victimize themselves inside their heads. They allow the Parasite to engage in self-deprecating litanies. These litanies include self-repudiation, self-punishment, self-hate, self-debasement, just to name a few. However, there is nothing trivial about the pain these litanies create in a victim. If you are engaging in any or all of the above, you are allowing yourself to remain a victim. You are allowing the Parasite to continue to recreate the pain of the abuse in you.

You are probably asking the following question: "So how do I become a survivor?" In AA, we hold that recovering is a process, rather than an event. In other words, you don't ever "arrive." Rather, it is a process of working at recovering one day at a time, one step at a time. In recovery, you make choices. Individuals choose not to drink today or at this particular moment in their lives. They may want a drink, or even feel they need a drink. They don't lie to themselves. They acknowledge their desire to drink. This is very important. Do not lie to yourself. You may want to (or even feel the need to) engage in your habituated self-abusive cycle. However, like the alcoholic, you desire healing more than further self-abuse. You choose healing over self-destruction, and you become empowered by that choice. This begins the cycle of healing. It will take time and much energy, but you can do it. It is your choice.

I have previously discussed the first and second steps of the Twelve Step Program. Let's review them. Step One: *We admitted we were powerless over alcohol—that our lives had become unmanageable.* Step Two: *We came to believe that a Power greater than ourselves could restore us to sanity.* In order to provide some clarity for us, let me alter these steps. Step One: "We admitted we were powerless over the pain of abuse—that our lives had become unbearable." Remember the paradox: "Power perfected in weakness." Step Two: We came to believe that a Power greater than ourselves could assist us in our healing." Now, I want to discuss the next steps.

Step Three: *We made a decision to turn our will and our lives to the care of God as we understand Him.* For our purposes, perhaps Step Three needs to be: "We made a decision to turn our pain and our lives over to the care of a Higher Power as we understand It." I know your trust in goodness has been shattered. However, I also know that it is critically important to work at restoring your trust in yourself, in others and in a Higher Power. I also know that there is great power in the phrase "Turn it over." When you feel completely overwhelmed and have no clue as to what to do with your pain, turn it over to your Higher Power. You need to work at leaving this pain with your Higher Power. Do not take it back!

AA recognizes that many people in recovery have a distorted image of their Higher Power. I know that almost all of my patients, past and present, have felt betrayed and abandoned by their Higher Power. I will discuss this in detail in another section. However, for the moment, I would ask you to appreciate that the Parasite is definitely at work here. It does not want you to connect with a Higher Power. It works to keep you away from this powerful source of healing. The Parasite will tell you that there is no Higher Power, no God. It will bait you into believing the Higher Power actually caused your abuse. No one can deny that this Higher Power allowed your abuse to happen. The Parasite will also tell you that you are not worthy to turn to a Higher Power. (*Worthy.* There's that bad word again.) I would simply ask you not to be fooled by the Parasite's nonsense!

Step Four: *We made a searching and fearless moral inventory of ourselves.* Again, for our purposes, I would like to rework this step. Step Four: "We made a searching and fearless moral inventory of the positive aspects of ourselves." You already know too well your weaknesses and human shortcomings. But, are you aware of the strengths and goodness that dwell in you? I have heard many people say: "I don't have any positive qualities." That is totally impossible, so please get to work on this positive inventory. Take a piece of paper and write down all those good qualities.

You need to make a firm commitment to curtail and eventually stop the self-abusive cycle. You need to begin to treat yourself with the respect and trust you need. You need to work the four steps I've just listed. When you commit to these aspects, you have begun your journey to become a survivor. I hope you had a chance to see the movie "What About Bob?" If you haven't, you really need to see it. I personally found it very funny and filled with paradoxes. The psychiatrist in the movie wrote a book titled *Baby Steps*. Psychology has for a long time used the phrase "Incremental Goal Attainment Scaling," or (as in the movie) the snappier "Baby Steps." This is how you need to journey to sur-viving—using Baby Steps. You need to go slowly and cautiously. It will be new territory. Take pride in your successes, no matter how small they may seem. You will be baited into minimizing your successes. Do not take the bait. Your success will give you power. You need that power to keep recovering.

My mentor, Guido D. Boriosi, M.D., is a psychiatrist whom I credit with my success in private practice. Dr. Boriosi wrote a book titled *Understanding Yourself, It's So Darn Easy*. In his book, Dr. Boriosi discusses the four P's to getting better:

1) Prayer
2) Pills
3) Patience
4) Push (p. 121)

Not that I know more than my illustrious mentor, but I would like to add another P for Persistence, and also change the order. So my Five P's are:

1) Prayer

2) Patience
3) Push
4) Persistence
5) Pills.

1. *Prayer*: Dr. Boriosi reports that this is self-explanatory and I fully agree with him.

2. *Patience*: Healing is a very slow process. Like physical healing from surgery or a debilitating illness, psychological healing is a slow process. There are no quick fixes. No matter how well you might progress, it will never be quick enough for you because you are in pain. You need to be patient.

3. *Push*: Pain—physical, psychological, or spiritual—is energy-depleting. Your fatigue is most real. However, you need to push yourself to do things even when you don't seem to have the energy.

4. *Persistence*: When you commit to working at a goal, you may not be completely successful. But you *are* working at it, and that can give you energy. When I began writing this book it felt like someone gave me a spoon and placed me on the beach at Wildwood Crest, New Jersey and said: "Get all the sand off the beach." My Parasite, (yes, we all have them), kept saying, "You'll never pull this off." However, I kept working at it and persisted in my goal.

5. *Pills*: The trauma of abuse is often associated with anxiety and mood disorders. Your therapist may have recommended medication to stabilize your neurochemistry and help reduce some of your symptoms. While I am not a Medical Doctor, my colleagues and I do know that medication can aid our patients in recovering. Psychotropic medications are slow-acting and they won't just heal you. There are no happy pills, but medication can be crucial to your recovery.

I well realize that I have placed a difficult challenge before you. Becoming a survivor is not easy, it does not just happen. I trust that you are feeling a sense of hope as well as a sense of empowerment. Take the first step. Begin walking the walk. Begin the journey of becoming—becoming a true survivor.

5

FORGIVENESS OF THE SELF

I know from my reading that many writers on the topic of abuse propose the need for forgiveness of the abuser. For these authors it is a way for the victims to diminish the valid anger, frustration, and hatred they feel for their abuser. The forgiveness of the abuser is actually directed at helping the victim heal. There are other writers on the topic who espouse the "Hang 'Em High" attitude. I am not proposing either approach. In fact, the question of forgiveness for the abuser is really beyond this text. From a faith-based notion, I believe my God's forgiveness is unlimited. However, while God's forgiveness is bountiful, one must first ask God for forgiveness in order to be forgiven. I might not be theologically sound, but I believe in the "Don't ask, Don't get" approach.

I know that my experiences are limited to the patients I have treated. However, to date, I have never treated a victim who has been asked by his or her abuser for forgiveness. If you have been asked by your abuser for forgiveness and you believe that it will aid you in your healing, then you need to work at forgiving the abuser. If you have not been asked for forgiveness, but believe you need to forgive your abuser in order to promote your healing, it is totally your choice. You need to do what is best for you. No matter what course of action you choose regarding your abuser, I believe an even more crucial issue, the forgiveness of the self, is where we need to focus our energies.

You may be thinking: "He has said time and time again that I am not responsible for my abuse. So why is he now telling me to forgive myself?" Allow me to explain. For a long time you have been involved in self-abusive behaviors. You have a part or parts of you that you believed were despicable. Some of your behaviors may have violated your own ethical or moral code. You may have held a part or parts of you responsible for your abuse. Yes, you were baited into doing these things to yourself by the Parasite. I know you didn't know better at the time. I know the intent was to simply get rid of your pain. Nonetheless, you abused yourself, and in order to reduce the ego fragmentation, the splitting of your psyche, you need to ask for and give forgiveness to the various parts of the self.

One of the best books that I have read on the topic of forgiveness is titled *Helping Clients Forgive. An Empirical Guide for Resolving Anger and Restoring Hope* by Robert Enright and Richard FitzGibbons. While the book is primarily directed at the process of forgiving others, it can be easily adopted to the forgiveness of self. The authors defined forgiving as follows:

> People, upon rationally determining they have been unfairly treated, forgive when they willfully abandon resentment and related responses (to which they have a right), and endeavor to respond to the wrongdoer based on a moral principle of beneficence, which may include compassion, unconditional worth, generosity, and moral love (to which the wrongdoer by nature of the hurtful act or acts, has no right). (p. 24)

As you can see, the definition can easily be reworked to encompass self-forgiveness. Throughout this book, I have challenged you to do many very difficult things. I know that self-forgiveness can be, and usually is, a struggle. However, it is an essential component of your healing.

Several months ago, I began working with Bridget, a twenty-nine-year-old medical secretary. She entered therapy for the treatment of panic disorder. Her history indicated that she was the fourth of six siblings. Her mother divorced her father three years prior to her entering treatment. Bridget reported that her father was a very angry man who had physically and emotionally abused her and her five siblings. She described her mother as a fragile woman who was quite loving. However, Bridget resented her mother for not protecting her and her siblings from the father whom she called the Beast.

Bridget had been dating a man she had met at work. From all indications, their relationship appeared quite healthy. They were engaged and planned to marry. During her fifth session, Bridget confided in me that three months after her engagement to "this great guy," she had cheated on him. She was certain that when she told him of her infidelity, he would break off the engagement. Instead of breaking off the relationship, he chose to forgive her.

Bridget told me that she had no idea as to why she was un-faithful. As it turns out, it appears that her Parasite baited her into believing her fiancé was too good for her. Unfortunately she took the bait, and was now even more convinced that he, in-deed, *was* too good for her. My clinical hypothesis is that this is a clear situation where the Parasite baited her into self-sabotage. I asked her if she believed he could and would truly forgive her. She responded, "Definitely yes!" Since she is a religious/spiritual individual, I asked her if her God forgave her. Again, she replied, "Yes." I then asked her if she would take her fiancé's forgiveness and her God's forgiveness and work at forgiving herself. She responded, "I don't believe that is possible." I explained that the Parasite is again baiting her into self-sabotage by her unwilling-ness to forgive herself. She then asked me how could I condone such behavior and expect her to condone her behavior as well.

I explained to her that I was not condoning her behavior, nor was I asking her to condone her behavior. I was simply asking her to forgive herself. She made a mistake. That mistake caused both her and her fiancé significant pain. She transgressed her moral boundaries. Nothing could take that back. What was done is done. She could not fix it.

She could not pretend it did not happen, but she could choose to forgive it. At this point in our therapy, she has chosen to work on the therapeutic goal of forgiving herself. It is for her a struggle and a long process. My continued hope for her is that she comes to accept her shortcoming and eventually forgive herself.

There are two words that need never be associated with forgiveness. One is forget; the other is condone. How many times in our lives have we heard the phrase "forgive and forget"? Well, the reality is that even when we chose to forgive, we don't forget. There are many things that happened to me in my lifetime. I have chosen to work at forgiving some of them. However, I haven't forgotten a single one of them. There are also many times when I have hurt people. I have asked for forgiveness and been given the blessing of forgiveness. Still, taking in that forgiveness and forgiving myself is a difficult task, especially when I listen to my Parasite.

When our daughter, who is now thirty, was less than a year old, she slipped and fell in the bathtub. I was the one bathing her. She wanted a bubble bath. The bubble solution was somewhat oily. At one point she stood up. I remember saying, "No, baby" and attempting to stop her from falling. She slipped through my arms, and hit the rim of the bathtub so hard that she drove her two front teeth back up into her gum. For years, this little girl went through dental procedure after dental procedure. Today, she has beautiful teeth and a beautiful smile. (Okay, I am biased.) However, that horrible scene still flashes in my head. I continue to work on forgiving myself.

I am hoping I have been able to convince you of the necessity of self-forgiveness. This inhibiting of self-forgiveness could be one of the last stands your Parasite can make in your war. Carpe Diem!

6

PERFECTIONISM AND PEOPLE-PLEASING

The concepts of perfectionism and people-pleasing have been previously mentioned in the section on development. However, both my research and treatment of victims of abuse have convinced me that these dynamic concepts play a significant Parasitic role in maintaining the self-abusive cycle. Unless these concepts are understood and given boundaries, true healing will be thwarted.

One of the most common traits of people who have been abused is their drive towards perfectionism. Since I have not had the privilege of meeting you and/or evaluating you, I cannot ethically say that you are a perfectionist. Chances are you are saying to yourself, "He obviously doesn't know me. I am anything but a perfectionist." All of my patients, to date, have said the very same thing. Please, hear what I'm saying, and be honest with yourself. Perhaps defining the term will help. The *APA Dictionary of Psychology* defines perfectionism as "the tendency to demand of others or oneself a higher level of performance than is required by the situation, thought by some to be a risk factor for depression." Perfectionism should not be confused with obsessive-compulsive disorder. Perfectionism also should not be confused with people believing themselves to be perfect already, which is commonly viewed as narcissism. Narcissism is "excessive-self love or egocentrism." I hope this helps clarify the concept of perfectionism.

Typically, victims of abuse feel that they are beneath most other people. The Parasite has been telling them exactly that for a long time. The Parasite has been saying things like, "You don't deserve to be her friend," or "You are not worthy to be in their company." I will give you a great example. I customarily shake hands with patients, male and female, as they exit my office (except in those situations when it is culturally or religiously inappropriate). For one young man, though, this common courtesy was a source of distress. Bill is a twenty-nine-year-old man who was abused physically and emotionally during childhood and adolescence by his alcoholic mother. He was abandoned at birth by his father. At the end of our fourth session, I went to shake Bill's hand. He said, "Please don't ask me to shake your hand; I am too dirty inside." After thirty-odd years in practice, I have heard many shocking things, but I was very taken aback by his statement, and by the pain I saw in his eyes. Bill, who felt too dirty inside to shake my hand, was a perfectionist.

Victims who are perfectionists tend to be very compassionate to others. They are typically very understanding of others' human frailties and can be quite forgiving to others. However, when it comes to themselves, they are relentless in their demands. There is no understanding, no compassion, and no forgiveness for the self. Perfectionists could receive ninety-nine compliments and one slight criticism in a given week. Can you guess where they will focus their attention? Where do you focus *your* attention? It seems like compliments, positive accomplishments, and successes bounce off them. But anything negative sticks to them like Velcro fasteners. Perfectionism creates a negative paradoxical effect: The harder you work at doing everything right the more you see what is wrong. My wife is a perfectionist. If you were to compliment her on how clean our home is, she will proceed to show you all the dust. She might even open our junk drawer to demonstrate how messy she is. If you compliment her on her dress, she will proceed to show you every pull in the fabric and then tell you she paid $7.00 for it at Kmart. I hope you are getting the picture.

Perfectionists have a tendency to catastrophize their human shortcomings. A tiny pimple on your forehead feels like you are growing another head. You spill a glass of water and you feel like you flooded your apartment. You go to a funeral home and get so nervous you thank the family for coming. Now you're convinced you are the dumbest jackass God ever created. And it only gets worse.

Because you judge yourself as being inferior, you set unrealistic goals for yourself. These unrealistic goals set you up for failure. As you fail in your goals, you continue to feel inferior. The more you feel inferior, the higher the goals become to compensate for your inferiority. Can you see the self-sabotaging process in this?

One goal that perfectionists typically adopt is people-pleasing. Their goal is to please everyone all the time. Do you see the total impossibility of this kind of goal? Let's go back to Bill. Despite the abuse Bill suffered from his mother, he feels an obligation to please her. Bill's fiancée, who knows his history, has a significant dislike for Bill's mother. During the Christmas holidays, Bill decided to take his mother and his fiancée to dinner and a movie. Bill's fiancée reluctantly agreed. During this great dinner at a very expensive restaurant, Bill's mother made some derogatory remarks regarding the fiancée. Bill was shocked, but said nothing. His fiancée was furious and left the table. Bill then said something to his mother who *also* became furious and left the restaurant. This occurred quite some time ago, yet Bill is still lamenting the situation. In his perception, because both mother and fiancée are still angry with him, the disaster is all his fault. The question I would ask you is: Is it all Bill's fault? Is it always all *your* fault?

Bill's Parasite played on his people-pleasing and perfectionism. He feels like a failure. The Parasite has even further baited him to take full responsibility for the disaster. He believes he must somehow do something for both mother and fiancée to compen-

sate for the disaster he caused. How can we help Bill? How can
we help you? Let us attempt to break this scenario down.

In the scheme of relationships, are we responsible for the
actions of others? Parents are, in my mind, responsible for their
young children. However, in order to grow into healthy adults,
the children eventually need to begin to take responsibility for
themselves. Certainly by mid-to-late adolescence, individuals
need to be responsible for their behavior.

In our relationships with other adults, I believe we are responsible *to* one another not *for* one another. This change in prepositions
(to vs. for) is not just semantics. It is a powerful mind-set altera-
tion. In our relationships, we impact one another both positively
and negatively. But does this impact then make us responsible for
others and what they subsequently do or don't do? I think not.
Suppose my wife and I had a horrible argument last night. (Of
course she started it and was totally wrong....just kidding!) I am
still hurt and angry the next day. Is she responsible for my abrupt
behavior to my patients and my students? I don't think so! Some
of my patients have recovered from their trauma and some have
not. Am I responsible for all their successes and failures? No. I
believe I must be responsible *to* them, not *for* them.

Similarly, Bill was not responsible for his mother's crude-
ness. Was he completely responsible to protect his fiancée from
his mother? I have said to Bill that perhaps he needed to support
his fiancée; however, she is an adult and needed to address the
situation as well. Granted, it was a most awkward situation. But
I don't think there was anything Bill could have done to prevent
the situation. Bill may need to come to terms with the fact that
his mother and fiancée will never become best friends. That is
really up to both of them.

For the longest time, Bill's mother has told him that she was
totally miserable all her life and that is why she drank. She has
also told him that it is his responsibility to make her happy. The
Parasite, using Bill's no-boundaries perfectionism and people-

pleasing baits him into wanting to do the impossible. No one can take responsibility for another's happiness. My wife is not responsible for my happiness. She can do and does many, many things to please me. However, it is her responsibility to please herself. It is my responsibility to make me happy. And it is no one's responsibility to do it perfectly.

I think we all know the serenity prayer: "Lord, grant me the serenity to accept the things I cannot change, the courage to change the things I can, and the wisdom to know the difference." There is much power in this prayer. Bill needs to accept he is a perfectionist and a people-pleaser. These aspects of his personality are good qualities when he maintains appropriate and consistent boundaries on them. He needs to accept himself and those around him as imperfect human beings. Bill needs to alter his expectations of himself and others. He can wish that his mother and his fiancée will become friends, but not expect it. He can wish he could fix them, but not expect that he can. He needs to change how he treats himself so he can say before his Higher Power: "I did my best. It was far from enough, but I did my best." When he can say that, he needs to give himself the same compassion, understanding and forgiveness he freely gives others. Alfred Adler, a theorist I have already mentioned, believed that "the healthy person has the courage to be imperfect because that is the normal state of human life."

It is important that you begin to balance your strengths against your human weaknesses. One way is to work at accepting compliments. Work to refrain from negating them in your head with the Parasitic "but" and "If you only knew." Keep in mind the AA slogan: "Fake it till you make it." Simply say "Thank you!" Once you become more comfortable with this step, the next step is to begin to integrate the compliments. I often ask my patients to make a deposit in their "heart bank." When you make a deposit in the heart bank or integrate the compliment, it acts as a reserve for those times when life becomes really difficult. Whenever I receive notes from patients or students that are complimentary, I save them in a particular file. During really low points in my life when I get down on myself, I will take them out and read some of them. Believe it or not, it really helps. Please, give it a chance. The only thing you have to lose is some of your pain.

Finally, I want to reiterate that the drive for perfectionism and people-pleasing are not unhealthy *per se*. Your drive for perfection has enabled you to succeed in a positive way. I know my drive for perfection enabled me to obtain my doctorate and to attain full professor status at my university. Similarly my people-pleasing drive has assisted me in evolving as a kind, compassionate, and caring man. No, those drives are not dysfunctional characteristics. They can and do provide us with the psychological energy necessary to succeed. Nonetheless, if these energy sources are not properly contained, they can lead to a meltdown. Consider a nuclear power plant. We take highly radioactive material and create a nuclear reaction. (Obviously, I am not a nuclear scientist.) This reaction, when properly contained, is an incredible source of energy. If it is not properly contained, though, a meltdown can occur, and a meltdown can be tremendously devastating. In an analogous manner, these characteristics of perfectionism and people-pleasing need to be properly contained.

Perhaps, throughout your life, you have experienced near meltdowns or actual meltdowns. A meltdown is when the perfectionist/people-pleaser says to himself or herself: "That's it, I'm through pleasing others! Screw everybody! I'm done with people. I'm done. Now, it's my turn. I'm going to do what I want, when I want to." Actually, this is not really you talking; it is the Parasite baiting you to swing to the opposite polarity. Operating from this polarity only creates guilt in you over time. You felt angry, frustrated, and resentful when you were striving for perfection and making people happy. But now that you have moved to the other polarity of pleasing only yourself, the guilt feelings are worse. The Parasite then baits you into swinging back again to the opposite polarity, only now, you must work even harder at being perfect and pleasing others in order to compensate. The Parasitic cycle continues in your striving for the impossible, while never really embracing the reality that these goals are impossible.

What you need to do is fully accept that these goals are impossible and strive for containment of the drives of perfectionism and people-pleasing. I view containment as setting appropriate limits and/or boundaries. You have not only a right, but also a responsibility to establish or re-establish boundaries. These boundaries are critical factors in healing and are also essential to healthy functioning. They afford us with a sense of control over ourselves and our behavior. After all, controlling ourselves and our behavior is really the only control we have in our lives. The next chapter will explore the concept of boundaries in depth.

7

Boundaries

This section might be a bit technical. I will work to KISS—that is, "Keep It Simple, Stupid." Please bear with me. If you have read other texts on the effects of childhood trauma or are currently in treatment, I am sure you have heard the words boundaries, boundary violations, appropriate boundaries, or limit-setting. Boundaries are essential aspects of healthy psychological functioning. Boundaries are crucial to our basic needs of safety and security, and therefore critical in the development of our sense of trust.

For clarity, may I define boundaries? The *APA Dictionary of Psychology* defines boundary as "a psychological demarcation that protects the integrity of an individual or group or that helps the person or group set realistic limits on participation in a relationship or activity." Perhaps it is important to examine this definition more closely. "A demarcation that protects" speaks to the notion of safety and security. Humans are very particular about their boundaries. If you own a home, I am sure you know the demarcation of your property limits. I am quite certain that you would feel violated if I started rummaging through your purse or your wallet. How uncomfortable do you get in a crowded elevator? Social psychologists would tell you that the discomfort you experience is a result of a violation of your spatial territory. Consider the resulting pain you experienced when someone violated the boundaries of your mind, your heart, and/or your body. Consider the horrific pain you experienced having your sense of safety and security shattered. Consider how this

violation impacted your ability to trust others and, more importantly, your ability to trust yourself. The trauma of abuse lies in
the boundary violation.

The boundary violation and the resultant breach in the child's
safety and security produces a feeling of complete loss of control in
the child. This feeling of loss of control is intense and completely
unbalances the child's sense of internal stability. The child, truly
unaware of the fact that you cannot make sense of non-sense,
begins to make sense of the abuse in order to regain equilibrium.
Here is where the Parasite really gains its power. Listen to some
of the power in the following statements:

"You are a lazy sack of shit. I wish we never had you."

"I would not have to drink, if I had a son I could be proud
of. But no, I got you."

"I did not want to beat you, but you had to push me, you
lousy shit."

"This is how little girls love their daddy. Don't you love your
daddy?'

"Don't you like making Daddy feel good?"

"This is how God wants me to show you love."

"I should have aborted you when I had the chance."

"I curse the day we adopted you. Your own biological mother
didn't want you. Do you know why? Well, I do. Because you
are a nothing!"

"Don't you like being special?"

Can you see all the contaminants in the water? Can you see
how the Parasite baits the child to absorb both the pain and the responsibility? Gestalt theory postulates the concept of introjections.
An introjection is when an individual swallows something whole
without chewing it. We need to chew on things, only ingesting
what is nourishing, while spitting out what is non-nourishing. It
is my contention that in abusive situations, children swallow both
the pain and the responsibility for the pain, as the whole introject.
Since children need nourishment (love), they have no recourse but

to keep looking to the abuser for their nourishment. The Parasite now is in power, playing various parts of the child's thinking and feeling. "I need to be very good tonight, so that Mommy doesn't drink. If I am good, Mommy won't drink and beat me. Mommy drank and beat me again. I am so bad. I'm sorry, Mommy, 'cause I am so bad. I'll be better tomorrow."

I know it is horrible! Yet, this is what keeps me writing, because I know you can do something to help heal this kind of pain.

Once the Parasite has baited or seduced the child into absorbing the pain and the responsibility for the pain, it forces the child into dichotomous thinking. Dichotomous thinking (sometimes called polarized thinking) is simply viewing the self, others, and/or the world as black or white with no in-between. "I am all bad and Mommy is all good. I need to be perfect. I need to please people all the time. I don't want to be selfish, so I must be selfless. I trust everyone or I trust no one."

Let us use an example. I have been treating Sally for five years. Sally, a thirty-four year old single woman, is the youngest of three sisters. When Sally was eleven, her mother died at home of a sudden massive heart attack. Sally was at home and witnessed the event. After her mother's death, her father became quite despondent and was emotionally unavailable. Then a male teacher began to take Sally under his wing. He was kind and told her he wanted to help her in her grief. Sally, being quite lost, took much consolation from being "special" to Mr. X. In time, Mr. X's special hugs became intense passionate kisses. Sally would freeze when this happened, but she needed his attention. One day, Mr. X took Sally to the janitor's closet. He opened his zipper and said, "Show me how much you like me." Sally reported to me that it was like she was there, but *not* there. "It was like I could see myself doing this to him, but I wasn't there." The trips to the janitor's closet continued until Sally was fourteen. It took her until then to have the ability to stop the insanity. Mr. X had his way with her orally, vaginally, and anally at least once a week.

Sally never told anyone. I was the first and only person to know of her trauma. Sally came to me shortly after reading of Mr. X's death in the paper.

Unfortunately, I have met numerous patients who have an intense self-loathing. Sally's self-loathing was the most intense I have seen to date. Sally told me that when she read of Mr. X's death, she felt relieved and happy. In her next statement, her Parasite said, "Now how sick is that?" I answered, "I don't think it is sick. I think it is quite human." Her Parasite in turn responded, "It's your job to patronize people, isn't it?"

At the time I met Sally she was grossly obese. Her Parasitic self-loathing triggered an excessive weight gain, which started at age fifteen. Her Parasite told her food was the only thing that could comfort her. No more confidants. No more friends. No more teachers. Her Parasite also told her that her weight would protect her. "I'm so fat that no one would ever want me. Besides, now I could not fit in the closet." She ate to feel comforted. The weight protected her. But she hated herself for being obese. So she ate to feel comforted for that. Do you see the Parasitic absorption of the pain and the responsibility for the pain? Do you see the boundary violation? Do you see the Parasitic cycle of self-abuse?

Obviously, Sally needed to realize her innocence in this traumatic situation. The disease, the Parasite, was relentless in pushing the fact that she knew it was wrong and yet did nothing to stop the abuse. The more I would ask her to examine the facts as she presented them to me, the more reasons the Parasite threw at her to hold her responsible. In our work together, I became convinced that therapy needed to be directed at the source of her struggle. Allow me to elaborate further. We worked on establishing the reality of the eleven-year-old. She had just lost her mother. Her father was emotionally unavailable. She was lost and very vulnerable. Eventually, Sally did concede and admit she would never hold another eleven-year-old responsible for what had happened to Sally. It appeared to me that this Parasite finally let go of that part of her. Then, we began to work on another aspect of the abuse: She was still responsible, in a way, because she enjoyed being special to Mr. X.

In my view of therapy and what I have described to you, I was using the "chemotherapy technique." We were in effect attacking the Parasite's hold on a part of her. As soon as we accomplished our goal, the Parasite would demonstrate its grip on another part. And the cycle continued. Pardon this next analogy—it was like being at an amusement park and playing the Whack-A-Mole game. As soon as we'd pound down one mole, another would surface, and on and on. Only, we were not at an amusement park, and it was not fun. Sally was in tremendous pain, and she wasn't getting better.

Sally and I had a discussion similar to the one above. Sally at first didn't like the metaphor of the Parasite. She did agree, though, that it felt like the Whack-A-Mole game. I suggested we needed to radiate the Parasite; that is, to identify what was truly Sally and what was her Parasite. Once we were able to identify the difference, she could radiate the Parasite in its "eye." This is accomplished by the patient's simply dismissing the Parasite as "stinking thinking" or the therapist's simply saying: "I won't talk to your Parasite." Perhaps it sounds too simple. It is not as simple as it seems. Remember the five P's. It demands much patience and persistence. You must keep radiating it and radiating it until it begins to shrink. Once you begin to perceive it shrinking, the hope of healing begins to truly root inside you.

The challenge for Sally (and perhaps the challenge for you) is to split the pain and the responsibility for the pain. The more I would tell Sally she was not responsible for her pain, the more she would say that she needed to be responsible for it. Then I said to her (about a thousand times), "You have held yourself responsible for the pain for the past sixteen years. You have punished yourself beyond belief. What good has it done? If you need to be responsible, then be responsible. You need to reestablish boundaries. Start by putting boundaries on the responsibility. Be responsible *to* your pain, not for it. Put boundaries on this sense of responsibility and use the energy that you have from that sense of responsibility to promote your healing rather than promoting self abuse."

Sally began to embrace the first three steps of the Twelve Step model. While it was very difficult for her to accept the disease model, she came to perceive the Parasite as her enemy instead of the psychological parts of her. Cautiously, she began to communicate with the various parts of her ego, including what she labeled the "eleven-year-old-girl." In these communications, she began to establish an agreement between the "eleven-year-old" and the other parts of herself to work at an agreement. Contained in this agreement was a commitment to use her anger to attack the Parasite rather than herself. This agreement allowed her to see that the "eleven-year-old part" and the "insatiable eating part" were not the enemies. Rather, she began to see that it was the Parasite that was the enemy. The Parasite played one part of her against the other, maintaining her ego fragmentation. The Parasite utilized this ego fragmentation to continue her self-abusive cycle. She actually embraced the dynamics of how the Parasite, using the self-abusive cycle to create her intense self-loathing, would have eventually consumed her. Sally's anger over her abuse became her best ally in attacking the Parasite. The anger she felt provided her with the necessary psychological energy to begin reestablishing a boundary within herself.

Eventually Sally took that subtle but powerful shift and began establishing a boundary on her sense of responsibility. She felt empowered, and she started shrinking the Parasite. She also began putting boundaries on her eating. In a year and a half, she lost a truly incredible amount of weight. "How much weight?" you might ask. I don't know. As much as I know about Sally and as much as she has shared with me, she will not reveal how much weight she has lost. When I ask, she smiles and says, "That's a healthy boundary, Doc, do not violate it."

Sally's situation exemplifies the need for the reestablishment of healthy boundaries. The boundary of being responsible to her pain allowed her to begin to trust herself. She learned a new word in therapy. That word is *no*. *No*, I don't have to be a doormat. *No*, I don't have to be perfect. *No*, I don't have to please everyone all the time. I can please people when I choose to please them. I can do my best and feel good about that, even when I don't achieve all I set out to achieve. Sally, in a slow but steady pace, began to see the "gray" in the world. More times than not, the gray was frightening, but not nearly as frightening as the black/white world her Parasite created for her.

Sally learned that selfish and selfless are polarities on a continuum. In order to avoid being selfish, an attribute she despised, the Parasite tricked her into being selfless. Her selflessness became a complete hell for her—a hell she had grave difficulty escaping. You see, whenever she said no to a person's request, she felt guilty. The Parasite told her that if she felt guilty, it must be wrong. So she quickly learned to never say no to anyone's request. Yet she found herself feeling angry and resentful of doing things for others.

I want you to know that I am not preaching a gospel for selfish people. I personally dislike selfish people. I will go out of my way to help people. When I choose to do something, it becomes empowering. When I have to, or I should, or I must, then it becomes a burden. That is when we begin to feel anger, frustration, and resentment. Webster's dictionary defines *selfless* as "having little concern for oneself and one's interest." It defines *selfish* as "caring only or chiefly for oneself; concerned with one's own interest regardless of others." It is clear that both polarities are unhealthy. Most developmental psychologists agree that balance is crucial to healthy functioning. Reestablishing pliable and intact boundaries is the key to balance.

8

FRAGMENTED, NOT DAMAGED

Throughout a significant portion of this book, I have repeatedly stated that you are not damaged. Perhaps you have said to yourself, "If I am not damaged, than what the hell am I? Because I sure feel like crap." I have already made several references to the Gestalt Parts Model. Healthy human functioning requires a fair degree of integration of the various parts of the ego. Trauma and/ or the introjection of contaminants results in ego fragmentation.

Trauma to a younger you is like a grenade suddenly exploding in your ego. The trauma—the explosion—came out of the blue, without warning. The various parts of the ego scrambled to ascertain what happened and why it happened. The trauma caused a total collapse of equilibrium. And then the Parasite appeared on the scene. In their increased alarm state, none of the parts recognized the Parasite as an intruder. Keep in mind that the Parasite was disguised as love. The ego was open to receive nourishing love; therefore, the ego defenses were down, with the various parts trusting that the ego would receive the nourishing love that is essential to the ego's health. The Parasite began to take charge. As it took charge of the crisis, it initiated the blaming of one part or another. The blaming—the making sense of the non-sense—began to afford the ego with a false sense of equilibrium. The trauma and the infestation of the Parasite resulted in ego fragmentation.

Let me emphasize this important part once more. The Parasite initially baits numerous parts of the ego into believing a part or parts of the self are responsible for the trauma. An ongoing war connived by the Parasite has been declared within the ego. There will be many casualties!

It only takes one episode of abuse or one traumatic episode for the contaminant to be ingested. That one episode is sufficient for the Parasite, with a mind of its own, to create ego fragmentation amidst the chaos of the trauma. Unfortunately, we know that child abuse is rarely, if ever, a one-time event. The more the child experiences trauma, the stronger the Parasite becomes. The stronger the Parasite becomes the more it connives to create more ego fragmentation, until finally the Parasite destroys any trust within and among the parts of the ego. With the parts of the ego at war, the Parasite is free to attempt an invasion of the psyche (or the soul) of the individual. The psyche contains the essence of the individual. If the Parasite breaches the psyche, the Parasite can and will eventually destroy the person psycho-spiritually and/or physically.

The more the Parasite tells you that you are damaged, the more this concept becomes rooted in your ego. The result is less self-worth, less self-regard, and less self-respect. This diminished self-worth, regard and respect only serves to intensify the war among the parts of the self.

Accepting and believing that your ego is fragmented but not damaged or broken is yet another crucial aspect of healing. You may be saying, "Is there really a difference?" There definitely is a difference. Allow me to provide yet another definition. Webster's dictionary defines *damage* as "injury or harm that reduces value, or usefulness." The Parasite has been taunting you with this word "damaged" for years. I know the patients I have worked with truly feel reduced in value. The Parasite has used this tactic over and over in your mind. It has, over time, truly convinced you that you are "less than" other people. Playing the various parts of your ego, you have developed your perfectionism and your people-pleasing characteristics in order to compensate for your sense of being damaged. (I have already discussed perfectionism and people-pleasing in detail in another chapter.)

Once you assimilated that you are damaged and accommodated by adopting perfectionism and people-pleasing to compensate for your damaged state, you were doomed to a vicious cycle. (Assimilation and accommodation are terms from the well-known child development theory of Jean Piaget. By assimilation and accommodation, the child internalizes awareness of the outside world.) Since you can never be perfect, or please people perfectly, the Parasitic notion of "damaged" was continually reinforced. This, believe it or not, is actually a quite normal adaptation to an abnormal situation. What I am saying is that considering the traumatic situation you endured, you, your ego, responded in a reasonable manner to adapt to an "insane" situation. The adaptive response is normal and understandable. Having been baited by the Parasite to adapt in this fashion, a child's or adolescent's ego simply could not comprehend the impossibility of this adaptation. In essence, while this adaptation was dysfunctional and served to create more and more pain for you, it was simultaneously quite functional on some level.

"So if I'm not damaged, what am I?" You are fragmented, or more accurately, your ego is fragmented. You might be thinking, "Here he goes with his word games again." No, that is truly not what I am doing. Remember, it is your Parasite that has played word games, and used these word games to create a vicious cycle of abuse and self-abuse. If you are going to "radiate it in the eye" you need to be equipped with more accurate data in order to counter the Parasite's games. "Fragmented" is very different from "damaged." Webster's dictionary in defining fragmented uses terms that include "an isolated part, or disunity." Clearly, you can see the definite difference in the terms "damaged" and "fragmented."

As I have already stated, the trauma created a fragmentation or disunification of the parts of your ego. Some of the parts of your ego actually blame some other parts of you for the abuse. As a result of this blaming, the Parasite has baited many of the parts of you to remove, exclude or contain the parts of the self responsible for the pain. When you stop and truly ponder this, it does make perfect sense. Remember the Biblical concept that if an eye is an occasion of sin, you must pluck it out. It is only logical, then, that if a part of me is responsible for all my pain, why not simply get rid of it? Then I won't be bad and I won't be in pain. This sounds logical to a child or adolescent who does not fully comprehend the impossibility of this kind of psychic surgery.

Many experts in the treatment of adult victims of abuse advocate healing the various parts of the self. An excellent book, *Healing the Child Within* by Dr. Charles L. Whitfield, has some very helpful information on this topic. I used many of that book's concepts in the treatment of my patients. Yet, without recognition of the existence of the Parasite and the games it plays, success was minimal at best. It is my theoretical position that, when you accept that you are fragmented and not damaged, you can and will need to utilize all the parts of your ego to battle the Parasite. You will need to communicate with the disunified parts. The Gestalt technique of Empty Chair is most useful in helping my patients communicate with the various parts of the self. Perhaps your therapist can help you with this technique: Sit about three feet across from an empty chair. Imagine that a part of your ego is sitting there. Talk to that part of your ego. Then shift to the empty chair to "speak for" the ego part. You will need to "make amends" with the part or parts of you that you attempted to exclude from your ego. I have addressed the making of amends in chapter five, Forgiveness of the Self.

9

God as Healer,
God as Persecutor

At the time I started writing this book, I envisioned this to be the last chapter. Maybe I saw it as the last chapter because I knew it would be, for me, the hardest. And, yet, I know it is one of the most important, if not *the* most important. When I was a rookie psychologist, I used to believe that when patients would talk about their sexuality, sexual intimacy or sexual encounters, they were revealing the most sacred aspect of themselves. Perhaps it is my increasing age, but I don't believe that at all any longer. I have now come to believe that it is when people talk about their spirituality, their relationship with a Higher Power or God, that they are talking about the most sacred part of their psyche. I want you to know that *I* know I am on sacred ground with you, the reader.

When I was in training in the 1980s, psychologists did not speak about religion, spirituality or God. It was as if those subjects were taboo. At some level, I believe that contributed to a rift between mental health and drug and alcohol professionals. Within the past ten to fifteen years, more and more psychologists have come to believe that the spiritual dimension of humans can be a key factor in promoting mental health. For many years, I have advocated to my students that they need to appreciate that humans exist in three spheres: physical, psychological, and spiritual.

In order to truly appreciate a human being, to study and to treat a person as a whole, we need to assess all three spheres.

While we are not medical doctors, psychologists typically obtain a full medical history on an individual. Why would we not obtain a spiritual history? In this book, I am not able to do that with you. If you are uncomfortable reading this chapter, I would advise you to stop at any point. But if you do stop, I would simply ask you to seek out a trusted clergyman to discuss your Higher Power or God. I believe that the Higher Power or the God that you relate to, the One you have a relationship with, can be a powerful healing agent. However, I have witnessed more often than not how the Parasite twists and distorts the image of a Higher Power until that Higher Power is nothing more than another abusive figure in the lives of the abused. If this is not the case with you, then, great. If this *is* a problem for you, please do something about it.

Any competent researcher will report the limitations of his or her work. I live and practice in a mid-size city in Northeastern Pennsylvania. The majority of the residents are Caucasian and aspire to Judeo-Christian principles. Currently, I have specialized my practice to include adult victims of abuse and members of the clergy, be they Protestant, Catholic or Jewish. It is important to note that the majority of my patients who are clergy, both male and female, have been abused as children. For the beginning of this chapter, I will use a portion of the article from the *ACA Journal*. I believe it lays some good groundwork. From this point on, I will refer to the Higher Power as God.

Spiritual Development

Victims' spiritual development parallels psychological development in that the process is highly adaptive but simultaneously very dysfunctional. Two key interplaying forces in this process are the transference of the parental image to the God image and the fixating at a mythical-literal stage of spiritual development.

The concept of imaging God based on the parental relationship was originally discussed by Freud. Andy Carey and I believe that effective treatment often becomes thwarted in the spiritual dimension, and that many therapists neither investigate nor attempt an intervention in this "sacred" spiritual domain.

In most religions, particularly the Judeo-Christian denominations, the image of God as Parent prevails. It's natural, then, for people reared in these faiths to develop concepts of God based on their experiences with earthly parents. During early childhood, not only is God imaged from parental experience, but mythical notions about God are also developed. There is a simplicity and security about this stage, and the literal interpretations seem to fit victims' black-white thinking.

For abused children, spiritual development is painful, frightening and highly conflicting. For them, God is a parent who will do anything "to make me good." God, like Mommy or Daddy, "wants what is best for me and only punishes me because He wants me to be perfect." These children assimilate that like the parent, God will love them some day when they have rid themselves of the evil and become worthy of His love. The spiritual relationship with God therefore necessitates "splitting defenses" on the part of the child in order to maintain a connection to the "Heavenly Parent." The self then is fragmented on both spiritual and psychological levels. The drive for perfection takes on a new dimension: "Not only do I need to be perfect to have God love me, but I need to make myself perfect to attain salvation."

As these abused individuals emerge into adulthood, they maintain the childhood notions and fears about God. God, in a mythical way, remains vengeful and conditional. In the victims' need to make sense out of their senseless experiences, they frequently view their pain and suffering as a "special blessing" from God. In the Judeo-Christian faiths, these victims hold firm to the principle of guilt and punishment, and often view their pain as a pathway to salvation. This dysfunctional bond with God is maintained in adulthood. Victims take the position that if any "good" occurs, it is because of God alone and not due to the individual's *cooperating* with God. Similarly, if anything "bad" occurs in their lives, it is solely because of their own flaws and behavior rather than any other possible explanation. As a result, these mistaken attributions serve to reinforce self-debasement.

Trust is obviously an essential component of faith and spiritual development. Because of victims' lack of trust, their spiritual development remains impeded and they remain stuck in immature stages of spiritual development. They stay spiritually bound in this relationship with God, demanding perfection of themselves. They are guilt-ridden about doing anything for themselves (typically viewed as being selfish). They are overly concerned about fulfilling the needs and wants of others, terrified by their own anger, and depressed by their emptiness. They desire an intimacy with God, but their perceived unworthiness prevents this from ever being experienced. Unless there is an intervention in this spiritual dimension, I believe that the wounds from their psychological trauma cannot heal.

As you are aware, I have addressed issues such as perfectionism, people-pleasing, and selfish vs. selfless in other chapters of this book. They are, indeed, very important in and of themselves. However, these concepts assume an even greater importance as they impact our relationship with God. Does God demand perfection? Does God demand that we selflessly please other people? Where was God when you were being abused? Where was God when his/her clergyperson said, "This is what God wants"? I only wish I could answer all of these questions with some definitive knowledge. I can only tell you what another human being thinks, feels and hopes are the answers.

1) "Does God demand perfection?" If there is a God, and He created us, then He above all knows we are imperfect and cannot achieve perfection. I find it very hard to believe God demands perfection. I believe He wants us simply to be the best we can be. I have told you before that I often say to my patients, "You know, if God uses the standards by which you judge yourself

to judge *me*, I don't stand a snowball's chance in hell of getting to heaven."

2) "What does God demand of me?" I don't think He demands anything of us. I often refer to what Jesus said in regard to the greatest commandment. He reportedly said "Love your God with your whole heart, and love your neighbor as you love yourself." Examine what Jesus said. Love God; love your neighbor; love yourself. You know I have been a Catholic for fifty-nine years. I have heard sermons or homilies on loving God and loving my neighbor, but I have yet to hear a homily on loving myself. Have you? Nonetheless, it is the third part of the greatest commandment. Did God create us just to be miserable? If you said, "Yes," I think that is your Parasite talking. Is God just a donor of pain and suffering? Did He put you here just so your parent could use you as a punching bag, or so someone could have his or her way with you? I know it may feel that way, but what kind of a God is that? Did God create disease, pain, and suffering just to test us? I truly believe evil created disease, pain and suffering. Evil thrives on pain. The person who abused you cooperated with evil and infected you with a Parasite. Now this Parasite taunts you into turning away from the only true source of unconditional love—the unconditional love that can aid you in destroying the Parasite. You know, in my youth, I was not convinced that evil existed. Today, I am as sure about evil existing as I am that I am putting pen to paper. I don't know why God allows evil to be so prevalent, so seductive, and so devastating. I am told it is because He gave us free will. Free will to the dumbest animals on earth! What was He thinking? (I truly hope God has a sense of humor.)

At this point, I would like to revisit the case of Sally. In examining her case, I will introduce the notion of Cognate God vs. Affect God. You may be saying, "What is he talking about?" I will explain. My work with clergy and victims has really come together in my finding that God is internalized in individuals on two levels. The Cognate God is the One we talk about, preach about, and want to believe in. The Affect God is the one we feel about, serve, and relate to. These concepts are, more often than not, very different representations of God. I have had patients who talk about a loving, forgiving, gentle, beneficent God. They can and do make God very attractive and most approachable. But when they really become honest with themselves and me, the Affect God is harsh, cold, demanding, vengeful, and an unforgiving SOB! And that is the God they relate to, the God they are supposed to trust. How can a Being like this give anyone comfort? He can't, and He doesn't, and that's the problem.

What I have not told you about Sally is her complete distrust of God. You see, she believes it was God who took her mom. Her image of God as Father was additionally compounded by her earthly father. When she needed a parent the most, he was totally unavailable. He was aloof, cold, and uncaring. Sally attended a religious-sponsored school. Mr. X, whom she thought to be her savior, was much respected both in the school and her congregation. He told her God wanted him to love her "that way." No wonder Sally's image of God is so horrible. Always keep in mind that the Parasite is playing these compounding facts. And here's the topper: After losing all the weight and truly working on healing, eight months ago God "gave her" a diagnosis of lymphoma.

When I first started working with Sally she reported herself to be spiritual but not very religious. This meant she believed in God but may not have prayed or have gone to church. Sally's Cognate God was quite impressive. He was gentle, loving, and very approachable. It was only after around two years of therapy that Sally started revealing her Affect God. She had refused to seek spiritual direction until approximately five months ago.

Sally's Parasite was completely fixated on this horrific God who took her mother, emotionally froze her father, and sent Mr. X to her. She was terrified of not being perfect for fear of what

God would give her as a punishment. Slowly and painfully, Sally began to forgive herself and worked at re-imaging her God. She utilized an image of God as mother rather than father. This shift was truly important and helpful to her, even though her particular denomination might frown on God the Mother. Her earthly mother had for the most part all the best characteristics of an earthly god. However, now her Parasite is working on the notion that her God the Father is punishing her for imaging Him as a woman. The war goes on for Sally. Can you hear what I am saying when I state that the Parasite has "a mind of its own"? More importantly, if you are to utilize the Twelve Step Model and invoke the assistance of a Higher Power, do you see why it is critical that your Affect Higher Power must be a source of consolation and not another source of pain?

Several years ago, I was working with a middle-aged woman who was sexually abused by her biological father and physically abused by her oldest brother. She was a Christian who was very scrupulous. Her Cognate God was, as expected, impeccable. Her Affect God was despicable. She could not relate to God the Father nor could she relate to God the Mother since her mother did not protect her. God the Son was mean, angry, and hostile and would punish her for not pleasing the Father. She was finally able to find consolation in God the Spirit. Thank God she believed in the Trinity!

The Twelve Step Model of a Higher Power is not religion. The concept of the Higher Power is not necessarily God, but rather a beneficent Being as you understand It. If God works for you, great! If God does not work, and you are able to connect with a beneficent Being, fine. If Higher Power fits better for you, that is fine also. Remember, the key is a Higher Power greater than yourself, however you understand It.

Looking back over my own life, I will admit I once had an Affect God that was conditional, vengeful and vindictive. I won't bore you with the details of why my God was so despicable, but there were some very understandable reasons. All of the theology courses and all of the homilies had very little impact on altering my perception of God. It was a very lengthy conversation I had with my dad and subsequent spiritual direction that helped me to begin to alter my perception of God. Growing up, my dad was not very religious. He didn't go to church much, but prayed daily. I have come to appreciate that while Dad was not religious, he was a deeply spiritual man. Dad was not highly educated since he only finished eighth grade, but he had incredible wisdom. Dad had what I now refer to as raw wisdom. One day, right after I had been notified that I had failed my second attempt at the challenging psychology licensing exam, I was watching our children. Dad came for a visit. I began lamenting about the exam and I was blaming God for my failure. "Why would God do this to me?" I asked of Dad. Dad's response was kind but stern. "Son, when bad things happen, don't blame God. You know, son, you and your sister have done things that have hurt me. You and Sis have done things to make me very angry. Yet, no matter what you have done, or could do, nothing would make me so hurt or angry that I would give you cancer or heart disease or make you fail your test. No, son, I would not do that and I'm just a fallible man who loves his children and wants them to be happy. Do you think God would love you less? Can you think of anything that your children, Mark or Mauri, could do to you that would make you just want to hurt them? Perhaps God does discipline us, but if He does, I'm sure He does it only to teach us. You know, son, the Father didn't crucify Jesus. Evil men did that!" What my dad said to me made sense. I hope it made some sense for you. Regardless, you need to be able to relate to a Higher Power that is a complete ally.

3) Where was God when I was being abused? Typical of a psychologist, I will answer your question with another question. Where was the Father when Jesus was terrified in the garden? Where was the Father when Jesus hung on His cross? I don't

have any definitive answers, but I can tell you what I believe. I believe the Father was in the garden, holding Jesus, consoling Him, wiping His tears. I believe the Father was at the cross, feeling His Son's pain with Him, whispering how sorry He was, telling his Son that He did not desire this. The Father knew it was going to happen and allowed it to happen, but never desired it to happen. I also believe this Higher Power, this God, is there with you every second of your life. Weeping with you. Feeling your pain and saying the same thing to you that He said to the Christ. "I didn't desire this to happen. I can take your pain. I will help you heal."

You may be saying, "But she told me this is how God wanted me to be loved." Unfortunately, many times what appears to be an angel of mercy turns out to be a resident of hell. You know, ever since humans have inhabited the earth, we have been doing horrible things to one another in the name of God. The tragedy the United States experienced on 9-11 was in the name of God. Holy Wars have been and are being declared in the name of God. Do you really believe this is what the God of humankind wants? Does it then surprise you that an elder of a church, a minister, priest, rabbi or sister would use the name of God to justify sin? Does that mean that God "ordained" your abuse? To me, it was nothing more than their sick and perverted justification for their sick and perverted act. Nonetheless, the sins are on them.

Many of my patients are very involved in AA, and I have attended numerous celebration meetings to support my patients in their sobriety. I have even been privileged to give my patients their chip celebrating their sobriety. I have heard many members' stories, particularly regarding their struggles with their Higher Power. Strangely, I found more genuine spirituality in these rooms than I have in any church. At one of those celebrations, I was asked to speak about my image of my God. I analogized God as being similar to Home Depot or Lowe's. God, like Home Depot, has everything we could possibly need to build a home. He will even deliver the materials to your site. He will put people—electricians, plumbers, and masons—in your life to help you. But He does not lay a block, sweat a pipe, or drive one single nail. That is all up to you.

I challenge you to build your house. He will grace you with what you need to accomplish your goal. If you are furious with Him, give your fury to Him. He's God; He will know what to do with it. If you can't trust Him, talk to Him about it. He's God; He already knows. Above all, work at never allowing a human, a religion, or a Parasite to come between you and your Higher Power.

A FINAL NOTE

We live in an incredibly fast-paced world. We can see live videos of situations happening around the globe. We can shop for an item online at three o'clock in the morning and have it in our possession within a day. The media is laden with advertisements of instant relief from pain of any kind. Even the advertisements for antidepressants make it appear that the depressed person recovers instantly. We have come to expect that everything in our lives should be instant.

To speak of patience is almost counterculture. Yet, the healing process of emotional, physical or spiritual issues is never instantaneous. The birthing process still requires nine months. A woman who is six months pregnant may become tired of being pregnant, and want to give birth today. No matter what the expectant mother wants, the fetus will not be born one minute before its time, so the mother needs to be patient. You will need to be patient with your healing process and with yourself. I know that for someone in pain, a minute or even a second is too long. However, patience is essential to effect true healing.

In addition to patience, I am going to ask you to examine the process of healing. In our Western culture, we have become event-oriented. We mark births, deaths, anniversaries, holidays as discrete events. Rarely, if ever, do we examine the process that often leads to the event. In healing, we really need to appreciate the process. I tell my students, over and over, that counseling is a process and not an event. Each session is like links in a chain, one building on the other to form the chain. If we go back to pregnancy, I believe it becomes clear that pregnancy is a process, not simply an event. Sure, it begins with conception which might appear to be an event. However, if we examine this closely, conception also includes the process of people falling in love, trusting each other, desiring intimacy, and so on. So, if you would, examine the process of pregnancy, following it from conception through all the steps and stages of the three trimesters to the actual birth. I think you get the point.

You have engaged in a process of healing. This process of healing requires patience, and necessitates that you fully engage in the process. If you were ever on vacation or on a trip with young children, you know that ten minutes away from home they start the "Are we there yet?" questions. Somehow that anticipation never really leaves us, even as adults. I am going to ask you to think in terms of the one day at a time, one moment at a time aspect for your journey in the healing process. I know you want to be healed, and you wanted to be healed yesterday. Now, we truly know that it is just not possible. Every day you awaken and choose to work at your healing; you are one step closer to your goal. You are one step closer to subduing the Parasite.

There will be days that you feel you took one step forward and three steps backward. You will inevitably feel defeated. Validate that feeling. But work at not allowing the Parasite to *overwhelm* you with that feeling. Remember, being on the journey itself, choosing life-giving behaviors over self-defeating behaviors is the essential aspect to your healing. When you fall, get up! Brush yourself off, work at forgiving yourself for being human, and continue on your journey.

As humans, we all have shortcomings, imperfections and frailties. Healing is a life-long process. Always know that perfection is a total impossibility. We must come to terms with being and doing our very best, and thus leave the rest to the Higher Power.

I said earlier in the book that some of the thoughts and concepts might seem redundant. I also told you that the redundancy was purposeful. Therapy and/or counseling is a redundant process.

It must be redundant at times in order to allow for the unlearning of faulty beliefs and the relearning of healthier, more adaptive beliefs. I believe that competent therapists rarely tell their clients things that the client, at some level, doesn't already know. The therapist's job is to tell the client things that the client can then see more clearly, or hear differently, or grasp onto in a more useful way. When you lose sight, or don't hear as well, or lose your grasp on your healing, it is often necessary to go over old material. That is normal and truly a part of the process.

This book was not written to be digested in one reading, or one week. If after reading it you found some concepts particularly useful, go back and re-read those pages. If you find yourself losing sight or sound, or a grip on something you want to work on in your journey, go over and over those pages until the concept sinks into your belief system. If you normalize your discouragement and validate those feelings, you can then focus your energy on this healing process. Keep your focus on winning the war, not every battle.

Shalom

SOME WORKS THAT HAVE SHAPED THE THOUGHTS IN THIS BOOK

Aber, J. & Allen, J. (1987). Effects of maltreatment on young children's socioemotional development: An attached theory perspective. *Developmental Psychology, 23,* 406-414.

Ainsworth, M. (1978). *Patterns of attachment: A psychological study of the strange situation.* Hillsdale, N.J.: Lawrence Erlbaum Associates.

Bohart, A. & Todd, J. (1988). *Foundations of clinical and counseling psychology.* New York: Harper & Row.

Boriosi, G. D. (2002). *Understanding Yourself, It's So Darn Easy.* Connecticut: Rutledge Books.

Bowlby, J. (1988). *A secure base: Parent-child attachment and healthy human development.* New York: Basic Books.

Berne, E. (1961). *Transactional analysis in psychotherapy.* New York: Grove Press, Inc.

Coker, L.S. (1990). A therapeutic recovery model for the female adult incest survivor. *Issues in Mental Health: Nursing,* 11, 109-123.

Erikson, E. (1963). *Childhood and society.* New York: Norton.

Enright, R.D. & Fitsgibbons, R.P. (2000). *Helping clients forgive an empirical guide for resolving anger and restoring hope.* Washington D.C.: American Psychological Association.

Festinger, (1957). *A theory of cognitive dissonance.* Standford, CA: Standford University Press.

Fowler, J. (1981). *Stages of faith: The psychology of human development and the quest for meaning.* San Francisco: Harper & Row.

Freud, S. (1955). Lines of advance in psychoanalytic theory. In J. Strachey (Ed.), *The Standard edition of the complete psychological works of Sigmund Freud* (Vol. 17). London: Hogarth Press. (Original work published 1918).

Groze, V. & Rosenthal, J. (1993). Attachment theory and the adoption of children with special needs. *Social Work Research and Abstracts, 29,* 5-12.

Inhelder, B. & Piaget, J. (1964). *The early growth of logic in the child, classification and seriation.* New York: Harper & Row.

Kohlberg, L. (1984). *The psychology of moral development: The nature and validity of moral stages.* San Francisco: Harper & Row.

Kushner, H. S. (1981). *When bad things happen to good people.* New York: Random House

Lau, E. & Donnan, S. (1987). Maternal and child factors for reported child abuse among Chinese in Hong Kong. *Social Science and Medicine, 24,* 449-452.

Lemoncelli, J. & Carey, A. (1996).The psychospiritual dynamics of Adult Survivors. *Counseling and Values, 4*(3),53-64.

Lynch, M. & Cicchetti, D. (1992). Maltreated children's reports of relatedness to their teachers. *New Directions for Child Development, 57,* 81-107.

Magid, K., & McElvey, C. (1989). *Children without a conscience.* New York: Bantam.

Mahler, M. (1968). *On human symbiosis and vicissitudes of individuals: Vol. I Infantile psychosis.* New York: International Press.

Mahler, M., Pine, F., & Bergman, A. (1975). *The psychological birth of the human infant.* New York: Basic Books.

Murdock, N., (2009). *Theories of counseling and psychotherapy. A case approach.* 2nd edition. New Jersey: Pearson.

Piaget, J. (1954). *The construction of reality in the child.* New York: Basic Books.

Schweitzer, R. & Lawton, P. (1989). Drug abusers' perceptions of their parents. *British Journal of Addiction, 84,* 309-314.

Sullivan, H. S. (1972). *Personal psychopathology.* New York: Norton.

Whitfield, C. (1989). *Healing the child within. Discovery and recovery for adult children of dysfunctional families.* Florida: Health Communications, Inc.

For more information about *A Mind of Its Own*, please contact Avventura Press at 570-876-5817 or email lee@avventurapress.com

www.avventurapress.com

Lightning Source UK Ltd.
Milton Keynes UK
UKOW01f1509300816

281804UK00001B/375/P